Increase Niles Tarbox

Missionary Patriots

Memoirs of James H. Schneider and Edward M. Schneider

Increase Niles Tarbox

Missionary Patriots

Memoirs of James H. Schneider and Edward M. Schneider

ISBN/EAN: 9783337307363

Printed in Europe, USA, Canada, Australia, Japan

Cover: Foto ©ninafisch / pixelio.de

More available books at **www.hansebooks.com**

MEMOIRS

OF

JAMES H. SCHNEIDER

AND

EDWARD M. SCHNEIDER.

BY
INCREASE N. TARBOX,
AUTHOR OF "BURIED CITY," "TYRE AND ALEXANDRIA," ETC.

BOSTON:
MASSACHUSETTS SABBATH SCHOOL SOCIETY,
DEPOSITORY 13 CORNHILL.
1867.

CONTENTS.

	PAGE
INTRODUCTORY CHAPTER,	7

JAMES H. SCHNEIDER.

I.—Birth and Early Years,	19
II.—Removal to Aintab,	31
III.—Removal to this Country,	48
IV.—School Days,	64
V.—College Life,	79
VI.—Connection with Normal School at Bridgewater,	98
VII.—Enters the Army. Ordained and becomes Chaplain,	118
VIII.—The Regiment ordered South. Goes to Ship Island,	138
IX.—Regiment removed to Key West,	159
X.—Sudden Death. Letters of Condolence,	183

XI. — Testimonials of Classmates and various
    Friends, ... 207

EDWARD M. SCHNEIDER.

I. — Early Years, ... 241
II. — Removal to this Country. School Days, . 263
III. — Enters the Army. Early Experiences, . 288
IV. — Killed in Battle, ... 315

MEMOIRS.

Introductory.

IN all the sad and trying years of our late war, if there was any class of American-born citizens whose hearts beat as the heart of one man for liberty and the national cause, it was the goodly company of American missionaries, scattered far and wide through the earth. At the last meeting of the American Board at Pittsfield, one of the Secretaries, giving an account of certain patriotic efforts of a missionary in former years, said sportively, "But the truth is, our missionaries, all the world over, are afflicted with patriotism, so that this may be accounted a chronic difficulty." From their lonely posts of observation in distant lands, — in the far East, in the Turkish Empire, in the islands of the sea,—as they looked on through these troubled years of conflict, they saw, even more clearly than we at home, the vast importance of a right decision. The questions at issue had with them, if possible, a deeper and more comprehensive meaning than with us. They saw that the influence of this land for good among the nations of the earth must be essentially lost, if the forces of evil should prevail and rend the great Republic. Educated men as they were, with large experience and observation, knowing the thoughts that were passing in the courts of kings and oppressors, as also among the poor and humble of the earth, they saw, almost as no other men could see, that it would be a dark day for the world, if the sun of freedom, shining over this western continent, should suffer a sad eclipse, and the hosts of slavery and rebellion achieve a triumph.

No more earnest prayers went up to Heaven for the good cause than those that ascended from these missionary dwellings in every part of the world. And more than this. The missionary churches everywhere caught the spirit of their teachers. In their religious assemblies, America, the land that had sent to them the Bread of Life, was never forgotten.

It was not strange, therefore, that the sons of missionaries, already in this land for purposes of business or education, or still living in their distant homes, should feel the patriotic fire burning within them, and should resolve, through peril and self-sacrifice, to defend the land of their fathers in its day of darkness and trouble.

It would be an interesting record, if some one, having access to the facts, would prepare a narrative in detail, giving the names of the sons of missionaries who served in our army in divers capacities, — some of them officers of high rank, and others in lowlier places, — and of the various fortunes that befell them. The purpose of this volume is to show what took place in connection with the family of one of these missionaries.

Rev. Benjamin Schneider, D. D., of Aintab, Syria, was a native of Pennsylvania. He was of German descent, but was educated in New England, graduating at Amherst College in 1830, and at Andover Theological Seminary in 1833. He was soon after married to Miss Eliza Abbott, daughter of Josiah Abbott, of Framingham, Mass.; and with his wife, in company with Rev. Thomas P. Johnston and wife, sailed from Boston, Dec. 12th, 1833, for Smyrna. On reaching that place, the little company passed on to Constantinople, arriving there in the month of February, 1834. When these missionaries left this country, it was expected that they would go together to the city of Broosa, which the American Board had just then resolved to occupy as a missionary station. But at Constantinople it was found expedient that the plan should be changed, and that Mr. S. and wife should go alone to Broosa. Accordingly, in company with Rev. Mr. Goodell,* — now the veteran and honored Dr. Goodell, — Mr. S. visited Broosa, and made arrangements for a missionary dwelling,

* Since the above was written, Dr. Goodell has passed away by death.

and, in July following, he and his wife took up their residence in this new field of labor.

The city of Broosa is situated about eighty miles nearly south from Constantinople, and was the chief city of the old province of Bithynia. Like many other ancient names, it has been subject to a great variety of spellings. It is called in history, variously, Brusa, Byrsa, Prusa, Brousa, Broussa, Broossa, and Broosa. The last is the form usually adopted by the missionaries. This was anciently, and is still, a place of great importance. It does not, indeed, come into view in the New Testament records, though it was in the same general region with the "seven churches of Asia." In the 16th chapter of Acts it is said of Paul and Timotheus in their journeyings, "After they were come to Mysia, they assayed to go into Bithynia; but the Spirit suffered them not." Though lying so near the scene of the great apostle's labor and travel, it does not appear that he ever visited this province.

In the days of Paul, all this part of the world, of course, was included in the great

Roman Empire, which then ruled with almost universal sway. But, after a few centuries had passed, this empire fell asunder by its own weight, and, in the year 328, under Constantine, there came to exist what is known in history as the Eastern Empire. This empire, with Constantinople (the city of Constantine) as its capital, though not without many outward wars and internal commotions, lasted more than a thousand years; but at length it began to be invaded from the East by the cruel followers of the False Prophet. On they moved, fired with fanatical zeal and hate. Little by little the empire yielded before their conquering march. Province after province fell away, and was added to the advancing kingdom of the Mohammedans. From generation to generation the war went on. At length, in the year 1326, Othman, the then leader of the invading hosts (who gave the name of Ottoman to the new empire), heard in his old age that his son Orchan had taken the city of Broosa, or Prusa, as it was then called. Gibbon says, "From the

INTRODUCTORY. 13

conquest of Prusa, we may date the true era of the Ottoman Empire. The lives and possessions of the Christian subjects were redeemed by a tribute, or ransom, of thirty thousand crowns of gold; and the city, by the labors of Orchan, assumed the aspect of a Mahometan capital. Prusa was decorated with a mosque, a college, and an hospital of royal foundation."

From this time on, for more than a century, Broosa was the capital of the Ottoman or Turkish Empire. Here the invading forces waited patiently to gather head for their last great and overwhelming attack, and in the year 1453, under the leadership of Mahomet II., the great city of Constantinople was taken, after an obstinate contest; sixty thousand of its inhabitants were mercilessly put to death; and the Eastern Empire was no more.

We have briefly recapitulated these facts of history, that it might be understood what kind of a place Broosa was as a field of missionary labor. More than any other empire on the earth, the Turkish Empire is one of mixed nationalities. In these central portions of the earth, around the early cradle of the race, conquest has followed conquest until the fragments of old nations are thrown confusedly together. At the time when the American Board made choice of Broosa as a missionary station, it contained not far from sixty thousand inhabitants. Of these, about six thousand were Greeks, belonging to the Greek Church; about six thousand were Armenians, having also their separate church organization; there was a smaller number of Jews, and a still smaller number of Roman Catholics. The rest of the population was mainly Mohammedan, the dominant population of the city and of the empire. Goodrich, in his "Pictorial Geography," writing at a later date, gives a larger population than we have named. He says of the place, "It is one of the most flourishing cities of the empire. It contains an ancient castle, a number of magnificent mosques, handsome caravanseries, and fine fountains, and has a hundred thousand inhabitants actively employed in manufactures and commerce. . . . It is the rendezvous of the caravans trading between Constantinople and the East, and contains many handsome buildings. Its cemeteries are remarkable for their extent and elegance, — the rich Turks of the European shore still preferring to be buried in Asia, out of love to the ancient land of their fathers."

The city is near the foot of that range of lofty mountains called the Mysian Olympus, and sometimes simply Mount Olympus; though the more famous mountain of that name, the fabled residence of the gods, is in Europe, on the confines of ancient Thessaly and Macedonia. But the Asiatic Olympus, skirting the borders of Mysia and Bithynia, rises proudly before the eye, and makes the region " rich in all the changes of beauty and grandeur." Near this spot is the ancient village of Nice, now called Isnik, a place of small importance in itself, but famous in history as the spot where the first general council of all Christendom was convened in the year 325.

It was in this city of Broosa, in July, 1834,

that the youthful missionary and his wife — most happily united in zeal for the great Master whom they served, and in readiness to do whatsoever their hands might find to do to promote his cause and kingdom — took up their abode. As missionary ground, the field was new; and difficulties of many kinds were to be encountered and overcome. But with faith in God, and animated with youthful hope, they patiently endured, and obtained the promises. Here they remained some fifteen years, until called in the providence of God to another and more distant field of labor. Here children were born to them. To tell the story of the life and death of two of these children — a story sad, but rich in precious memories — is the object of the present volume.

JAMES H. SCHNEIDER.

CHAPTER I.

BIRTH AND EARLY YEARS.

JAMES H. SCHNEIDER was born in Broosa, Asia Minor, on the 14th of March, 1839. He was the third child in a family of five,— two daughters and three sons. So soon as he came to years of observation, he looked out upon a crowded and bustling city, filled with strange sights and sounds. As has been already stated, the predominant population of the city was Mohammedan. This is the religion of the empire, of which the city is a part; and consequently, both by reason of numbers and the favor of the government, this form of religion displayed itself with more openness and show than any other. Here were costly and splendid mosques; here the great fast and feast days were kept with noisy and imposing ceremonies, and everywhere the eyes and ears were assailed with the rites and forms and usages of the followers of the False Prophet. But there were also in the city some six thousand inhabitants of the Greek Church,—a Christian population in name, and only in name. Like the rest of those great organizations into which the Christian Church, in the early centuries, became divided, it had the form of godliness, but denied the power thereof. Almost every vestige of evangelical piety and true spirituality had long ago died out from it. In the early years of Dr. Schneider's missionary life, his labors were chiefly among this Greek population.

There were also in this city some six thousand Armenians, members of the old Armenian Church, whose origin dates back to the fourth century of our era. Then it was, when Constantine having declared the Roman Empire a Christian state, that apostles of the faith went forth in various directions, and, among the rest, Gregory the Enlightener, as he was called, who carried the gospel to the Armenians, and laid the foundation of this Armenian Church. Meanwhile, as the centuries had been rolling away, these Armenians, broken up in their own land by war and conquest, or stirred by desires of traffic and gain, had become mingled up with the various races thrown promiscuously together in the Turkish Empire. In the early days of our Turkish missions, there was more expectation of success in missionary labor among the Greeks than among this people. But by degrees it was discovered that the minds of the Armenians were far more susceptible to the influence of vital Christianity than any other people in the empire; and the later labors of the American Board in that quarter of the world have been mainly among the Armenians. Every one at all acquainted with foreign missionary operations knows with what an encouraging, and even wonderful, measure of success these labors have been attended. But, as we have already said, when Dr. S. first went to Broosa, in 1834, it was more especially his business to carry the gospel to the Greeks.

There were at that time in the city three synagogues of Jews; for, in every place almost throughout the world, where traffic is going on, this remarkable race is to be found. And especially in all those central portions of the earth near to the ancient home of these children of Abraham, in every city and village almost, Jews, in greater or less numbers, are almost certain to be found. And, as has already been said, there was a small element in the population of Roman Catholics. One third or one fourth part of the population was therefore Christian in name; but, in all the city, at the time our missionaries went there, there was almost nothing that was Christian, according to the pure and simple standard of the New Testament.

Surrounded by such outward associations as these, young Schneider passed the early years of his life. Writing, as we do, so far from the place of his birth and so far from those who would retain many of the incidents of his childhood, we shall be compelled to leave this part of our narrative less fully developed and illustrated than we could desire. His father says of him, " As to incidents in his early life, none of a peculiar nature marked his childhood. He was kind and gentle in his disposition, and gave his parents less care and anxiety, probably, than children usually do. . . . His education, before he went to America, was mainly in the hands of his excellent and

BIRTH AND EARLY YEARS. 23

beloved mother (now dead). From the pressure of missionary work resting upon me in this great field, I could give him and my other children but imperfect attention in this respect; and hence the intellectual training of these sons fell chiefly upon her. By the energy and activity of her character, she was enabled to do more in this particular than most persons would have thought possible. Still, with the cares of her family and the share she took in our missionary work, the children could not have the same amount of intellectual care which those of a similar age in America usually receive."

In this modest passage, Dr. S. has probably undervalued his own influence and agency in the formation of the character of the children, while those who were acquainted with their mother will bear witness that he has not overestimated hers. She was, in many respects, a woman of rare qualities of character, — energetic in her household and in outside missionary work; full of zeal and courage for the Master; with such a kindling element of imagination in her nature as to keep her buoyant and hopeful when clouds were dark, and when many women, far from their home and their native land, would have been sad and discouraged, and would have given themselves up to vain repinings. For these early years of missionary labor in the Turkish Empire were by no means years of security and ease. Protestants had no real protection for themselves from any quarter, while they were among a people proud and self-confident, and able to throw perpetual obstacles in the way of the missionary. The Turkish Government had been compelled to grant a kind of toleration to the different Christian sects of the empire, so that the religious affairs of the Armenians were in their own hands, and others must not interfere. So with the Greek Church, the Roman Catholic, the Jews. If the Greek Church wished to punish a man for leaving its fold and going over to the missionaries, the government, in those years, said, virtually, "We have nothing to do with this matter; the Greek Church manages its own religious affairs." As a consequence, the missionaries were subject to endless interference in their work, and they had nothing to do but to possess their souls in patience amid endless provocations, and look to Heaven for wisdom and strength.

In the absence of such incidents as we could desire for the better illustration of these early years of young Schneider's life, it may be well for us to gather a few facts and incidents from the early communications of his father to the "Missionary Herald." These will help to show the character of the city in which he lived, and what was taking place at that early period, when his eyes were first opened to watch the scenes that were going on around him. We shall cull these without any particular reference to dates, with the simple design of showing what the life of a Christian missionary in the East then was, and what must have been some of the thoughts and feelings of a quick and observing boy in the midst of such an uncertain and tumultuous life.

When Dr. S. first visited Broosa, in company with Dr. Goodell, the common people seemed pleased with the idea that a missionary was coming to reside among them, and arrangements were readily made by which a dwelling was hired for a residence. But when Mr. and Mrs. S. came to Broosa to take the dwelling, he found, " that the Greek bishop had commanded his people not to furnish us a house until he had written to the Patriarch of Constantinople about it, at the same time threatening to use his influence with him to interpose his authority. But the owner of the house, being a man considerably enlightened, would not be deterred by the menace of the bishop. The house was his, and he would dispose of it as he saw fit. If any one wished for it, he would give him the use of it at his own pleasure. . . . Thus we have been permitted to settle down quietly under our own vine and fig-tree, grateful that we have a shelter, remembering that our Saviour had not so much as where to lay his head."

The following picture shows that his lot was now cast among the " habitations of cruelty " : —

" As I walked out to-day, I saw several young Turks led along the streets with their hands tied. They had just come from a neighboring village, where they were taken by force and surprise to be made soldiers.

On one occasion I saw fifty or more linked together, two by two, drawn along the street like so many criminals. They have just been torn from the embraces of their families, perhaps never to see them again. . . . When soldiers are needed, each village must furnish a number proportioned to its population. Whoever happens to be in the street is apprehended and brought bound to the place of rendezvous. Thus they proceed till the requisite number is obtained."

The following will help the reader to catch a clear conception of the scenery surrounding the plain on which Broosa stands: —

"To-day ascended Mount Olympus in company with Mr. Merrick and Mr. Powers. We started early in the morning, having wrapped ourselves in warm clothing for the cold atmosphere of the mountain. As we began to ascend, the sun had risen a little above the horizon, giving a beautiful appearance to the city. Notwithstanding the unfavorable exterior of Turkish edifices, the view was charming. How much more so would it have been, if Philadelphia (the modern American city), with its regular streets and fine buildings, had .

been spread out to our view. Indeed, if Broosa were in the hands of an enlightened and Christian nation, it would become a paradise. . . . The pleasure of planting our feet upon the highest point of Olympus was an abundant compensation for our toil. From this eminence the scene was truly sublime. . . . The difference between the thermometer on the top and at the bottom of the mountain was thirty-two degrees, it being sixty-two below. . . . Not long since the height of the mountain was taken by a French gentleman. According to my informant, who was present when the measurement was taken, the altitude is eight thousand feet above the sea."

Such a mountain, as it is seen in winter and summer, in storm and sunshine, — when the first rays of the morning kindle it, and when the light of the setting sun plays around its snowy summits, is in itself an everlasting storehouse of influences, not only material but æsthetic and spiritual. All the operations of nature around these mountain heights are on a scale of majesty and power. No wonder that the ancient dwellers in these lands, with their wild mythologies and superstitions, should people these dizzy summits of the world with beings of imagination.

"To-day commenced the *corban beiram*, a feast of Mussulmans continuing four days. . . . It derives its name from their custom of observing a sacrifice (corban) on the first day of the feast. Immediately on leaving the mosque, after the morning prayer, the victim must be sacrificed. Every Mussulman who is able to purchase a sheep is bound to obey the custom. When they are poor, several unite, and defray the expenses together, while the rich kill from one to five and sometimes more. It is supposed that in the city from twelve thousand to fifteen thousand sheep were slain, probably all of them within one hour."

As the years were passing away, every now and then flames of opposition and persecution would be kindled by the authorities of the Greek Church. Some school of fifty, sixty, or seventy scholars would be suddenly broken up and scattered, and all the books used by the school would be gathered together and burned. Bibles and New Testaments, distributed among the people, would share the same fate. Nevertheless good was done. The word of God made triumphs, and, though it was the day of small things, as compared with Dr. S.'s later days of missionary life, he did not faint nor grow weary. The family remained here until the early part of 1849, when James was ten years old.

CHAPTER II.

REMOVAL TO AINTAB.

IN the year 1849, Dr. Schneider removed from Broosa to Aintab, in Northern Syria. The two daughters at this time were placed at school in Constantinople, while Mr. and Mrs. S., with the three boys, went to Aintab.

The occasion of this removal will be well remembered by those who have followed, from year to year, the history of the operations of the American Board. As early as the year 1844, a religious movement began among the Armenian population in Aintab and the region round about, of a truly remarkable character. In that year, Dr. Azariah Smith, of blessed memory, made a journey to Mosul, and, in going and returning, he twice passed through this portion of Syria, and found among the people a remarkable susceptibility to religious truth. On his return to Beirut he sent a native colporteur, with the Bible and other religious books into those parts, and these were taken with wonderful avidity. This was in the year 1845. In 1847, Rev. Mr. Van Lennep visited Aintab, and performed some missionary labor, though his imperfect acquaintance with the language was a great hindrance to him in his work. In 1848, Dr. Schneider made a journey thither, and found things in a most hopeful condition. Up to this point of time, the main influence exerted upon the people had been through the Bible and religious books, and not through the voice of the living preacher. Yet Dr. S., on making his visit there in 1848, writes: " There is now a permanent congregation of one hundred, and the prospect of a gradual yet constant increase is highly encouraging. You must not be surprised if there shall be, within a year or two, a congregation of two or three hundred, or even more." In the winter of 1848, a Christian Church was formed at Aintab, and during the year 1848, Dr. Smith was requested to make his residence in this part of the country, and take charge of the Armenian department at Aleppo and Aintab. As already stated, in

May, 1849, Dr. S. joined him, and from that time until the present, Aintab has been the scene of his labors, where the Lord has wonderfully prospered and blessed him in his work.

If one will look upon the map, he will find Aintab a little way in the interior from the north-eastern point of the Mediterranean Sea. In a straight line, it is not distant perhaps from the sea more than sixty miles. But by the route usually travelled from the harbor of Scanderoon the distance is about ninety miles.

In Aintab, the Armenians formed a large element in the population. At the time Dr. S. went there, he estimated their number at ten thousand. The city is not so large as Broosa. Another missionary reckoned the whole number of dwellings in the city at four thousand, of which the Armenians had fifteen hundred. These Armenians of Aintab, and throughout all this section of the Turkish Empire, were far more honest, sincere, simple-hearted than those in Constantinople and its vicinity. The Armenians of Constantinople were one hundred and fifty thousand in number, and though they had had much missionary labor bestowed upon them, the gospel, at this time, had gained no remarkable triumphs among them. But they of Aintab and Aleppo, and in the surrounding country, were more noble than those in Constantinople, "in that they received the word with all readiness of mind, and searched the Scriptures daily whether those things were so." When the Bible was first circulated there in 1845, they were prepared to receive it, and when the labors of the day were done, they gathered in little circles, night after night, to study the Scriptures. They were "not far from the kingdom of heaven."

After reading the Bible for some time in this way, they became intensely desirous that a religious teacher should come and remain among them, and they could hardly endure the delays and hindrances, until this was accomplished. In 1847, they received the joyful news that Mr. Van Lennep was coming. They heard of him at Aleppo; but as he did not arrive at Aintab so soon as was expected, one of their number wrote a letter, which he and sixteen others signed, and which was ready to be despatched to Aleppo, when Mr. Van Lennep arrived in person, and the epistle was put into his hands. The expression "holy one," which occurs in it, is after the fashion of the old Armenian Church, when a priest or preacher is addressed. Our missionaries do not encourage the use of such language. We give this letter, as showing the state of mind among the Armenians of Aintab before any missionary had gone to reside among them.

"It is now sixteen days, O holy one, since we sent you a letter; and neither have you made your appearance, nor has an answer come to us. It is evident, holy ones, that you have laughed at our beards. If you intend to visit us, come on; if not we must look after a preacher for ourselves and ask one of God. These sixteen days have been sixteen years of anxious expectation. This is wrong, brethren.

"Why have you thus long kept away from us? We have been contending alone against the world. We have fought against the whole city, until only three men and a half remain against us. Why are you so careless? When will you come? If you behave so, we shall have to write to Constantinople; we shall have to write to Smyrna for a preacher.

I write no more, but hope to speak with you face to face in Aintab. Holy ones, I have written little but understand a great deal. Stop not any longer by the way; reach this place by Easter."

Rev. Mr. Van Lennep remained but a short time at Aintab, because of his imperfect acquaintance with the language, and was succeeded by Rev. Mr. Johnston. There were, of course, the same essential elements of society here as at Broosa, though mingled in different proportions. The Mohammedan part of the population was less when compared with the whole, and the Armenian greater. Here, also, were Greeks and Jews and Catholics, and other Christian sects such as abound in all this part of the world.

Aleppo is the capital, and the great centre of trade for northern Syria. It lies south from Aintab a distance of seventy-five miles, and contains a population of 150,000. The general configuration of the country in these parts may be understood by remembering that the lofty double range of Lebanon (Libanus and Anti-Libanus) runs along near the shore of the Mediterranean, through nearly the whole length of Syria, so that for a distance of many miles back from the sea, the country is extremely rough and mountainous. Beyond these mountain ranges, one looks out upon that broad and level plain, — the early seat of empire, which figures so largely both in sacred and profane history. A traveller, starting, for example, from the ancient city of Damascus, which is some three hundred miles south of Aintab, and journeying northward toward the latter city, will see all the way this Lebanon range towering on his left or westerly side, while far away on the right will stretch this vast plain of the East. He will follow along the course of the river Orontes, which is fed by the streams coming down the easterly slope of the mountains keeping its track near their base, until it reaches the city of Antioch, where it makes a sudden bend to the west, and, through a pass in the mountains, pours its waters into the Mediterranean. Aintab is not out upon this level plain, neither is it in amid the fastnesses of the mountains.. It is in the hill country where these mountain ranges are spreading out, and fading away to the north.

Rev. Dr. Anderson, late secretary of the

American Board, in his journey to the East, in 1855, passed through this region, and spent two Sabbaths at Aintab. A few extracts from his letters home will give the reader a clear idea of the place and of the great work then going on. Dr. A., coming from Aleppo, reached Aintab on Friday.

"A little past noon on the third day, five or six miles from Aintab, at least, a score of native brethren met us on horseback, with Messrs. Schneider, Pratt, and Beebee. Their cordial greetings affected us. When we set forward, our native brethren preceded us, singing the hymn, in Turkish, —

"'How sweet the name of Jesus sounds,' etc.

And sweetly it did sound from such voices, as we rode along. Just before reaching the city, they again sang, —

"'When I behold the wondrous cross
On which the Prince of Glory died,' etc.

We soon felt ourselves to be in one of the great centres of missionary influence; and every hour has strengthened this impression. Kessab is but an outpost to Aintab."

He describes Aintab as "built upon three hills, rising from a valley and running east and west." On the central hill, not quite so high as those on either side, is the church. "The building is of stone, with alternate layers of white and black, and is eighty-two feet by fifty-nine. It has a gallery on three sides, and will seat fifteen hundred persons." We omit certain items pertaining to the history of the building, the manner in which the ground was secured, etc., and pass on to his description of the Sabbath in Aintab.

"Sabbath was to us a great day. The bright beams of the sun were attempered by the autumnal breezes; and the surrounding stillness, owing to the absence of business from this part of the town, allowed us the full enjoyment of our hallowed privileges. First came the Sabbath school of sixty boys and seventy-six girls, superintended by a native theological student from Marash (which is becoming a station of great promise), and taught by six males and nine females from the native church, — Mrs. Schneider and Mrs. Pratt having each a class of the older girls. The dress, order, and manner of the school were all that could be expected, and even more."

. . . . .

"Public worship commenced at eleven. Here we saw an audience of seven hundred people, all seated upon matting on the ground-floor. The lower part of the church was well filled,— the women being under the gallery on the north side, and rather crowded, and the men, composing two-thirds of the audience, occupying the rest of the space. The men took off their slippers as they entered, and deposited them on shelves made in the wall under the windows; and the women did the same with their loose yellow boots. The dress was entirely oriental. With the males there was considerable variety, with a taste for strong colors; but the whole person of the female, including the head and part of the face, was covered with a well-adjusted white muslin, as large as a sheet, which is supposed to be the veil worn by Rebecca, Ruth, and other women of ancient times in this part of the world. I found it hard to realize that the large audience before me was actually Protestant. Such, no doubt, is the fact, excepting the few strangers. Mr. Schneider preached from Rev. v. 12, ' Worthy is the Lamb,' etc., with animation and feeling. The aspect of the audience was eminently Christian. They also gave good attention in the afternoon, when most of my own discourse, kindly interpreted by Dr. Pratt, was composed of facts illustrating the recent progress of Christ's kingdom. That is a kingdom in whose prosperity not a few of the hearers had a deep sympathy.

"On my way from church, I was interested to perceive how exactly Mr. Calhoun's feelings tallied with my own. Neither of us has heretofore realized the greatness of the work here; and now the appropriate emotions found no easy utterance. The results would have seemed great after the labors of an age; and scarcely nine years have elapsed since the first missionary visit was made by Mr. Van Lennep, and scarcely eight since Mr. Johnston was expelled from the place with tumult and stoning."

. . . . .

"The city of Antioch, once numbering its hundreds of thousands, was long one of the grand centres of the Christian world. For ages past, Aleppo has been the prominent city of Northern Syria. But the present Christian centre of this part of Syria is Aintab. For this section of country it is the Antioch of our day. The members of the church would perhaps be lightly esteemed by the more polished Aleppines, and still more in the great metropolis; but they are chosen of God, a royal priesthood, and are a blessing to thousands."

Though there was, as we have said, a remarkable eagerness, on the part of many of the Armenians of Aintab, to hear the gospel, yet there was also a fierce spirit of opposition and persecution on the part of the old Armenian Church. Indeed, this spirit of opposition, all the world over, is apt to be in proportion to the energy and success with which the real work of the gospel is going forward. Even in Christian America there is nothing like a powerful revival of religion to awaken the hatred and spite of many unconverted men. Before Mr. Schneider went there, this flame of persecution had been kindled, and, as suggested in the passage from Dr. Anderson, Rev.

Mr. Johnston had been driven out of the city by a violent mob, which not only made use of hard and threatening words, but of stones also. When we consider what poor human nature is, it was not wonderful that this feeling of jealousy and hate should be kindled among the Armenian church-leaders, when they saw their people leaving them to follow new guides. It required, therefore, in the early days of the gospel work in this city, great wisdom and discretion, so to conduct affairs as to avoid an outbreak of this tempest of wrath. The missionaries knew well that these wild elements were all about them even when they were not let loose, and they needed to be " wise as serpents and harmless as doves," to prevent agitation and public alarm.

At this place, the subject of our memoir lived three years, from the spring of 1849 to the spring of 1852. He was subject here to much the same outward influences as at Broosa, only he saw the gospel here making much more rapid progress than at his former residence. He saw his father and mother both engaged most industriously, feeding the hungry souls about them; for one of the peculiarities of this work at Aintab was that the gospel wrought as powerfully among the women as the men. This, of course, in our own land, would not be strange; but it was strange there. In all these Eastern countries, women are made to occupy such a subordinate place in society, that they are perpetually kept in the background, and no public movement of any kind is expected to reach and affect them as it affects the men. But at Aintab the women also received the gospel, and Mrs. Schneider, who was herself of a most elastic and enterprising nature, gave herself with all her energies to the work of instructing these Armenian women intellectually and spiritually. The missionary dwelling was a place of constant resort by inquirers after the truth. By day and by night they came to learn of Jesus and the great salvation. It can never perhaps be known what effect was wrought by all this upon the minds of the three boys, who were passing their childhood in the midst of these scenes,— what thoughts were awakened within them,— what seed was sown to bear fruit in after years.

While living at Aintab, these children became subject to a curious disorder that prevails in that part of the world, but which is more severe at Aintab than in any other place. Dr. Schneider describes it as follows: —

"In Aintab, and many places in these regions, there is a singular phenomenon in the form of an eruption in the shape of a boil. It is called by Europeans the *Aleppo button*, because they first met with it in that place; but it is much more virulent in Aintab. This boil or sore appears in childhood in the case of natives of Aintab, and generally in the cheek. No one escapes it, and every child has at least one, and very often three, four, five, or more. From its commencement to its healing up, a year passes, and hence it is called by the natives *the year sore*. I have often seen the faces of children completely covered with this sore. It is not particularly painful, except when it is brought violently in contact with something. After healing up, a scar is left, and by that a citizen of Aintab may be recognized in any part of the world. We parents and our three sons all suffered from this eruption. I could not wear a hat for six months or more because of three of these large sores on my forehead; though I could use the Turkish fez. James had an unusual number of them, — his face, neck, hands, and all the exposed parts of his body being covered with them. I sent the water of five or six different springs, and several specimens of the rocks of Aintab to Dr. Hitchcock, of Amherst College, for analysis, hoping that the cause of this phenomenon might be discovered; but the analysis revealed nothing whatever as to its origin."

In addition to what Dr. S. has thus written, we may relate, what we have heard from his own lips, that, if this sore is left entirely untouched to work its own course, no very perceptible scar will remain; but it is subject at times to an intolerable itching, and a child cannot usually have patience to let it alone. Moreover, it is exposed, especially in the case of young children, during the long period of its continuance, to many accidental collisions, by which the covering or scab is disturbed and the scar is left. With adults, as in the case of Mr. and Mrs. Schneider, where there is reason to guide, and where the necessary precautions will be taken, the scar is hardly noticeable.

It seemed suitable here to make mention of this peculiar disease, because it had not a little to do with young Schneider's thoughts and feelings during all the early years of his life in this country. Naturally modest and bashful, he had, at times, especially among strangers, a painful sense of a certain injury or deformity wrought upon his face by this strange disorder. As he came to know himself and the world better, this feeling gradually passed away, and in his later years it hardly entered his mind, at least as a painful or disturbing element.

CHAPTER III.

REMOVAL TO THIS COUNTRY.

THUS far in our narrative, by the very necessities of the case, the subject of this memoir has not come prominently into view. We could do little more than give a few leading facts in his early history, and show the general surroundings by which his character was shaped and moulded. From this time onward the case will be different.

One of the troublesome and painful questions, which missionaries in every part of the world have to encounter and settle, pertains to their children. Wherever a foreign missionary is sent to labor, the fact itself presupposes a state of society wicked and corrupt. People sometimes please themselves and amuse others with long discourse about the natural goodness of man. But the great outstanding fact respecting this world is that it is a world of sin and rebellion against God. In no place upon the earth, except where the gospel has done its work, can even a fair standard of outward morality be found. And, indeed, there is no land as yet beneath the sun where the gospel of Jesus Christ has so thoroughly penetrated and prevailed that the wickedness and corruption of human society do not plainly appear. But the difference between a land like our own beloved New England, where the gospel has wrought as effectually perhaps as anywhere else in the world, and any country subject to Paganism, Mohammedanism, or even some form of corrupted Christianity, is so great and manifest that no candid observer can fail to see it in a moment. In all the savage and half-civilized portions of the world, where our foreign missionaries are sent to labor, the forces of evil are in the ascendency as they are not here. Sin and wickedness in manifold forms stalk abroad. They are not so careful as here to hide themselves behind some veil of concealment.

The consequence is that our missionaries, especially in the early years of their labor in any place, and before they have been able to shape society somewhat to a Christian standard, do not feel that they can freely expose their children to the evil influences about them. A system of isolation and seclusion has by a kind of necessity to be largely practised, that their little ones, with their fresh, opening minds, may not see the sights or hear the sounds of that noisy world of wickedness around them. They are kept as strictly as may be within the enclosures of the parental nest, where the father, and especially the mother, may watch over them and guard them from these evil contaminations. But this system of restraint cannot continue beyond a certain period. The growing boy, with his restless, active nature, must have freedom. His wings are grown, and he must enjoy the liberty of flying abroad. The girl can be kept longer secluded. Especially in the East, where all the habits of society are in that direction, it is not difficult to keep the missionary daughters more within the enclosures of home. But neither for the sons nor daughters is this seclusion in itself to be desired. They need to be at large, where they can breathe the free air of heaven, and catch the healthy and invigorating influences of a broader and more generous existence.

Hence missionary fathers and mothers, in whatever part of the world they may be laboring, as they see young children gathering about them, have to meet the question, What shall be done with them? Hard as it is to be separated, the desire for the well-being of the children almost always prevails, and they are sent back to the early home of the parents for education. When we consider all the hazards and uncertainties naturally attendant upon such a state of things, it is wonderful that so few evil consequences have followed, and that the general result of this long-continued experiment has been so eminently good. It seems as if God had wrought by a special providence in behalf of these his servants, who, to promote his cause and kingdom, had taken their lives in their hands and gone to the ends of the earth. When we look over this whole chapter of missionary history in connection with the American Board, reaching on now more than half-a-century, out of this long course of providence we seem to hear God speaking, as distinctly as he spake by word to Abraham of old, saying, "I will establish my covenant between me and thee and thy seed after thee, in their generations, for an everlasting covenant; to be a God unto thee and to thy seed after thee."

Many missionary children, it is true, have died at so early an age, that no such questions needed to be raised respecting them. Over all the earth are scattered little graves, where our missionaries have laid their young children to rest, and gone back to their solitary dwellings to mourn without the sustaining sympathy of kindred and friends.

The present Mrs. Schneider, in one of her letters a few years since, at a time of great mortality among the little children of the missionary families in the East, said, "Over all Syria is there a voice heard of weeping, lamentation, and mourning, Rachel weeping for her children."

But hundreds of these missionary children, from various parts of the earth, are alive today, bearing an honorable part in the activities of the world, and not a few of them are back in the various missionary fields to take the places of their fathers. As has already been stated, many of these missionary sons served in the loyal army during the late war, and no one of them (we speak of the children of missionaries of the American Board), — no one of them was found in the ranks of the rebellion. We make this latter statement on the authority of one of the speakers at the late meeting of the Board, who from his associations ought to know, and who said, that "not one of the children of our missionaries has proved disloyal or has had to apologize for treason."

In the spring of 1852, it was felt that the time had come when the question of the children must be met and decided. Accordingly, Mr. and Mrs. Schneider, with the three boys, proceeded to Smyrna. There, according to previous arrangement, they were met by the two daughters, Susan and Eliza, who had been brought thither from Constantinople, so that the little flock were together again, after a three years' separation. From the port of Smyrna Mrs. Schneider embarked for America with four children, Susan, Eliza, James, and William, leaving Edward (or Eddie, as he was familiarly called, — not then quite six years old) to return along with his father to Aintab. The life of this little boy — as he then was — is to be unfolded in the second part of this volume; but we may here say a word about the affliction which came upon him from this separation, and the story can best be told in the simple and touching language of his father: —

"This separation from his mother and brothers and sisters was most painful to him. He was almost inconsolable. After bidding them farewell in Smyrna and embarking on the steamer to return with me to Aintab, his childish heart seemed almost to break. I shall never forget those sorrowful hours. My own heart being full of grief by this separation from my loved ones, I was poorly prepared to offer him consolation. In making the effort, I could hardly control my own feelings, and felt that I needed some one to give me comfort, rather than labor to dissipate his sorrows. He finally wept himself to sleep in his state-room, but a deep sadness followed him for a long time. One of the painful sacrifices, to which the missionary is often called, is thus brought into view, — this separation of parents and children, for the purpose of their obtaining an education in America."

One fact, very honorable to his own Christian patience and fidelity, Dr. Schneider has not here mentioned. He was himself expecting to come to America at this time with his wife and children. The German Reformed churches of the Middle States, then associated with the Board, of which Dr. S., by race and early associations, was a kind of representative, had requested that he might come home for a season, and impart to them the lessons of his experience in the missionary fields where he had wrought. It was accordingly arranged that Mr. and Mrs. S., with the children, should come to America about this time. After nearly twenty years' absence from kindred and native land, it can easily be imagined with what longings the heart would turn towards home. But the sudden death of Dr. Azariah Smith, and the very promising and hopeful condition of things at Aintab, made him feel that it would not be right for him then to leave, and he remained behind. If the reader will add this fact, and the feelings naturally growing out of it, to what Dr. S. has above stated, it can then be understood with what mingled emotions he returned, with his little son, to his lonely home in Aintab.

Rev. Dwight W. Marsh, then returning from missionary labor in Mosul, now at Rochester, New York, gives the following graphic description of the parting at Smyrna, and the voyage home: —

"In the Gulf of Smyrna, with steam on, the 'Vapore' was chafing at her anchors, ready to bear Mr. Schneider and his little Eddie back to Syria. In Smyrna he had just parted from Susan, Eliza, James, and William, and their mother. He asked me into his state-room, gave a few last charges and prayerful commendations, stretched out the parting hand, then turned and gave way to not unmanly tears.

"I had been in his family at Aintab, also in missionary conference at Beirut, had brought Susan and Eliza from Constantinople, and now, under God, he had committed them to me for the Mediterranean and the Atlantic voyage. I had reason to feel a solemn responsibility.

"A few days later, like Columbus, and as confident, we started for the setting sun. With his sisters, who were a few years older, James shared in good degree those golden dreams of the New World which, to an American child born in the Orient, are visions hardly less clear than the revelations of the Paradise above.

"But we had something better. Jesus was with us in the ship. When a mutiny occurred, just out of the Straits of Gibraltar, and a bloody knife was plunged into the breast of our mate, did we not seem to see our Saviour rise from his pillow, and hear him say to furious passions, Peace, be still? We believe that he anointed the eyes of some of those sailors and enabled them to see his glory. James, too, in particular, thought that he then gave his heart to God. He conversed freely with me; but I was led to think that he had previously, at Aintab, accepted the offers of mercy. However that may be, I have no doubt that he was then under gracious influences of the Holy Spirit, that he felt his lost condition by nature, repented of sin, and savingly trusted in the only Saviour of men.

"This was to me the great fact of the voyage. God was keeping promise. He answered prayers of the faithful absent father, and prayers of the faithful present sisters and mother. This presence of God with James was of itself enough to bring angels down; and for many days they hovered round our white-winged bark with tender solicitude."

They had a long passage of seventy-seven days before reaching the land of their fathers, arriving here in mid-summer, 1852. James was now in his fourteenth year, his birthday falling in March. His father writes: "It was during this voyage that he became deeply concerned for his salvation. He came to his mother in great distress of mind, asking her what he should do. The counsel she would give him can be easily imagined. I think he dated his conversion from that period."

On reaching America, there were many kind hearts to welcome Mrs. S. and the little strangers. There was the hospitable Christian home in Framingham, from which Mrs. S. had gone forth, nearly twenty years before, in the bloom of youth, and where her parents, now advanced in life, were still living, and who were ready to "rejoice with exceeding joy" at the sight of a beloved and honored daughter, from whom they had been so long parted. There was the kind Aunt Susan, as the children called her, the youngest sister of Mrs. S., and the only one of her father's family then remaining at home. Thickly scattered through all the region were the relatives, as also the early associates and friends, of Mrs. S., — all waiting to extend the hand of greeting, and bid her a cordial welcome to her old home.

Full well does the writer of this remember the pleasant sight, which he first had, of this missionary-mother : full of life and energy, with her beautiful group of children about her, — the two daughters, soft and gentle in their aspect and manner, just blooming into womanhood; the two boys, retiring and bashful, but far more hopeful and attractive than if they had been forward and bustling. It is one of those pictures not easily effaced from the memory. With all their exposures to the unhealthy climate of the East, with all the various hazards of travel by sea and by land, death had never entered this family circle, and it seemed like a little garden which the Lord had blessed. Though these children had not been favored with such opportunities for education as they would have enjoyed in this land, yet they had been kept under such choice Christian influences that there was something very pleasing in their quiet and respectful demeanor in the presence of strangers; and it was easily discovered, by inquiry, that they had used well their powers of observation, and were furnished with a large share of useful and valuable information.

The daughters, having never been at Aintab, had not been scarred with the *Aleppo button;* but the two boys, and especially James, showed the marks of this singular disease very distinctly. There was nothing, perhaps, in his conduct and manner, at that time, which would reveal the fact that he carried within him a painful consciousness of these scars, — only his modesty and bashfulness were very noticeable. There are a great many boys in this country, of about the same age he was then, of whom it may be said, that if they could be kept modest, could be held a little in the back-ground by some such disorder, all their friends and acquaintances would have reason to regard it as a wholesome and merciful infliction.

Soon after the children reached their grandfather's house in Framingham, Aunt Susan, — the present Mrs. Schneider, — having a decent regard for appearances, and wishing the young folks to be as presentable as possible, was asking Mrs. S. if something could not have been done to prevent these scars upon James's face. Mrs. S., whose consecration to her work was of a truly heroic character, promptly replied, in substance, " When I consecrated myself to the missionary work, I consecrated my children, also; and I expected them to share the fortunes of life in those places where the Lord should see fit to send us."

The first few months after the return must naturally be occupied in greetings and friendly reunions. Not only were there many friends in Massachusetts, but the kindred of Dr. Schneider, in Pennsylvania, must also see these comers from the East. There were brothers, also, of Mrs. S., with their families, who must be visited. It was natural, therefore, that some little time should elapse before any systematic arrangements would be made respecting the education of the children.

For the sake of giving the reader a clear conception of the relations of persons and places at this time, and thus shedding light over the subsequent parts of the narrative, it seems best that all formality of authorship should be for a moment dropped, and a brief and simple statement be made.

[I was at that time living in Framingham, where, from 1844 to 1851, I had been pastor of the Hollis Evangelical Church, of which Mrs. Schneider's family (the Abbotts) were members. After leaving the pastoral office for my present work, I still made my residence for several years at Framingham. In the spring of 1852, not far from the time when Mrs. S. and the children left Aintab to return home, Rev. J. C. Bodwell (now Dr. Bodwell, professor in the Connecticut Theological Institute at Hartford) was installed pastor at Framingham. Rev. Dr. Dutton and his wife, of the North Church in New Haven, Ct. (now both gone to a better world), were wont, year by year, during Mr. Dutton's vacation in August, to visit with us at Framingham. Soon after Mrs. S.'s return, it so happened that she and her children were invited to our house during the visit of Mr. and Mrs. Dutton. Out of this circumstance, probably, grew the arrangement afterward made respecting the education of the two daughters. In Saxonville, a village in the north-east part of Framingham, Rev. B. G. Northrop (so long the efficient agent of the Massachusetts Board of Education, and now the Secretary of the Board of Education in Connecticut) was at that time pastor of the Congregational Church. The home of the Abbott family was about midway between Saxonville and Framingham Centre. Mr. Northrop at once became acquainted with these children on their coming to this country, and has since greatly befriended and aided the boys in their education. His house has been a kind of home for them.]

CHAPTER IV.

SCHOOL-DAYS.

IN this chapter we must pass somewhat rapidly over a period of about four years, extending from the fall of 1852 to the fall of 1856. Many events of great importance, in the history of this little missionary household, occurred during this period. But we must not forget that this is a memoir of one member of the household, and our narrative must keep itself mainly to the development of the story of his life. That which happened, however, in his own circle of kindred and among his near and dear friends is, in truth, a part of his own history; for his quick affections took hold of these passing events with such earnestness and tenacity as to shape and control his inner life. While we are following him, therefore, through these four years, we shall not lose sight of the important changes and events that are going on around him.

After due inquiry, for the purpose of making choice of a school at which James might be advantageously placed, — the element of expense being one important item in the calculation, — it was finally decided that he should go to the academy in Thetford, Vt.; and here he commenced systematically his course of study and education. Hitherto, as has been already stated, his education had been broken and irregular. His father and mother had done what they could, and the result was highly creditable to their patience and fidelity in the midst of their pressing public duties. But now began the work of thorough and continuous mental training.

The two daughters, Susan and Eliza, were placed at school at New Haven, at Grove Hall, then, and until recently, under the charge of Miss Mary Dutton, sister of Rev. Dr. Dutton, of the North Church. The place was every way desirable, opening to them the amplest opportunities for culture and society, and Miss D. made the terms so easy and generous that the offer was gladly accepted.

William, the youngest of the four who came to this country, was to return to Aintab with his mother, when her visit should be completed. She remained in the country not far from a year; saw the three elder children safely and happily located; visited her own kindred and those of Dr. S.; received the joyous hospitality of many Christian people in different sections of the country, who knew well her works and labors of love; took leave of her aged parents, whom naturally she could no more hope to see in the flesh, and sailed with her son for her distant home, reaching Aintab in the fall of 1853. There she found an abundance of work awaiting her, "so mightily grew the word of God and prevailed." The Protestant congregation at Aintab had already passed far beyond the sanguine expectations expressed by Dr. S. when he first went upon the ground, though he regarded the field, even then, as exceedingly hopeful. It had come to be numbered by several hundreds, and has since increased to such an extent as to make a division of it necessary.

Once at regular study, James discovered an

aptitude for superior scholarship. His faithful attention to his books, the accuracy of his recitations, and the guilelessness and simplicity of his manners, soon won for him the high regard of his teachers. They became strongly attached to this lad, who, far away from home and parental restraint, conducted himself with a manly wisdom and discretion, and by his devotion to books showed that he had in him the true spirit of a scholar.

He remained at Thetford about two years, when, for certain reasons, it was thought best that he should leave that school, and enter Phillips Academy, Andover. Here he came under the care of S. H. Taylor, LL. D., now for many years the head of that celebrated institution, and who has had the care of fitting as many young men for college, probably, as any other living teacher in this country. The aims of this academy have always been high. In the classical department, especially, the discipline has been accurate and severe.

Here young Schneider found himself upon a broader platform of study. He was brought into competition with a much larger number of minds, and, in any well-regulated school or college, this friction of mind with mind among the students is one of the most important elements of education. If a young man comes to such a place puffed up with family pride, or swelling with his own inherent vanity, he is very apt to get the conceit taken out of him. If he comes bashful and retiring, and finds by degrees that he makes his mark among the multitude, — reaches a high and honorable standing in scholarship, — confidence in himself is imparted, and he becomes master of himself and the situation.

The latter was emphatically the condition of young Schneider. He did not think better of himself than he ought to think. He was well aware that his advantages had been few, compared with those enjoyed generally by the young people of New England. He had a very humble idea of his personal appearance, and attached an undue importance to the disfigurings upon his face. He needed encouragement rather than repression. Self-confidence and boldness, which in so many boys are in excess, in him were lacking. His life at Andover did much for him. It gave him courage. His rank as a scholar was so high, even on so large a scale of comparison and competition, that he began to feel the use of his powers, and to forecast, not vainly, but wisely, what he might be and do.

Rev. Mr. Northrop, who stood to him, in these years, somewhat in *loco parentis*, and who understood well what was wanting for the development of his best powers, was mainly instrumental in effecting the arrangement by which it was made possible for him to enter Phillips Academy.

As has already been stated, it was during his voyage across the Atlantic that the conviction came upon him of his state and condition as a sinner before God, and of his need of pardon and cleansing by the blood of Christ and the regenerating and purifying influences of the Holy Spirit. It was then, as is believed, that he first caught a vivid conception of that higher standard of character, revealed from the holy law of God, and before which " every mouth must be stopped and all the world become guilty." Though young in years, simple and guileless in the eye of earthly judgments and standards of character, yet his senses were quickened to discern spiritual realities, and he saw and felt that in him there was really no good thing, but that God, through Christ, was waiting graciously to renew and sanctify his soul and plant in it the seeds of holiness.

But has one so young and comparatively innocent any occasion for such experiences as these? That is what the world often asks; but these are things that the world knoweth not of. The late Rev. Dudley Tyng, of precious memory, while yet a boy of about the same age of young Schneider at the time of his conversion, came one night to the study of his father,— who was engaged in some writing that occupied him at the midnight hours,— and, stealing quietly into the room, when he was supposed to be locked fast in slumber, said, "Father, I am so sinful that I cannot sleep." Is there any man whose senses are so dull to divine things that he argues anything weak and foolish in such an experience of a youthful soul and this frank confession of it? Can any man resist the conclusion that a soul so sensitive to evil is made for noble ends, and that it is already beginning to forecast its range and destiny?

Compare an experience like that of this child
— revealing itself in this manner in the solemn
midnight hours — with the utter thoughtless-
ness and apparent inability to appreciate such
things often seen in boys of the same age, and
will any man have the audacity to say that the
latter is the more hopeful state and condition
in respect to character, either for this world
or another? Nay, Heaven bends with a loving
interest over such a child; and men, bad as
this world is, in spite of themselves, bend toward him, drawn by a nameless charm which
they cannot resist. Young Schneider had
these emotions awakened in him when out on
the lonely ocean, beholding "the works of
God and his wonders in the deep," and he
came to his mother with the story of his convictions. She, who had guided so many
blinded and bewildered souls in Turkey to
the Lamb of God, was eminently fitted, by
grace and by experience, to guide her own
darling boy — her first-born son — to the same
precious Saviour. We cannot doubt that his
religious life began from that point. Such
is his father's impression. Such was his own
impression, given to those to whom he imparted these hidden secrets of the soul.

But he was young, and it was well that there should be some delay before he made a public profession of his faith in Christ. There was more than usual religious interest during the time of his stay at Thetford, and his spiritual impulses were deepened. An advance was made in the divine life. While at Andover, he felt that the time had come when duty to God, to his fellow-men, and to himself, required that he should make a public profession. And it was a nice and delicate impulse that moved him, if it might so be, to connect himself with the church in Framingham, of which his own dear mother was a member, and where she had received her early Christian nurture. Application was made accordingly, and it need not be said that the church most joyfully accepted the proposal. We will leave to Rev. Dr. Bodwell, who was then pastor, and who kindly consented to furnish a paper embodying his reminiscences of the event, to describe more fully this interesting scene : —

"I remember well the day on which our dear brother, James Schneider, united with the church in Framingham. It was the first

Sabbath in February, 1856. Many will recall that winter as having been remarkable for severity and for deep, drifting snows, which had not melted all away when April came. The New Year's sacramental service had been deferred by reason of the weather. A heavy, driving snow-storm on the first Sabbath in January had made it very difficult for anybody to get to church, and there was no service. The following Sabbath was a brilliant day, though very cold; but a heavy fall of snow on Saturday had been blown into such deep and solid drifts that travelling was out of the question, and again there was no service.

"The first Sabbath in February was bright and beautiful, cold and still. The attendance at the morning service was large, as it was known that six persons were to be received into the church on profession of their faith, — all but one being young, — three of them young ladies and two young men. Moreover, there was a very tender affection for James Schneider in the church and congregation; for many who were present on that day remembered the time when his sainted mother had stood there, and taken on herself the same solemn vows in the freshness of her maiden beauty. It was also the church of his revered grandparents and all their goodly household of sons and daughters. The father of James, the Rev. Dr. Schneider, had greatly endeared himself to the congregation by his interesting reports of his labors and his appeals on behalf of his people at Aintab. And, what was still more, perhaps, a strong sympathy in the cause of Christian missions had been awakened and cherished in that church by their having given two much-loved members to the work, — the Hon. Peter Parker and Mrs. Schneider, — who had labored so successfully in two of the most interesting and important sections of the great missionary field.

"The congregation in whose presence James Schneider stood up to take on himself vows of Christian consecration saw in him, as they thought, the future missionary to far distant lands. It was well understood that his character for native talent and fine scholarship, not less than for a beautiful combination of modesty and sweet temper and warm affection, with a decision and manliness which excited respect even at so early an age, gave rich promise of honorable service and eminent usefulness in any sphere to which God should call him.

"It was the custom of the church at Framingham to give the full time of morning worship to the sacramental service, a brief address taking the place of the sermon. The congregation was frequently larger than was usual on other days, especially when members were to be received, and no one retired till all was concluded. When, after the reading of the Confession of Faith and the Covenant, the pastor, as was his custom, gave to James, in his turn, the right hand of fellowship, and addressed him directly on the great step he had taken, there was a breathless stillness to catch the main incidents of his conversion as they were interwoven in the brief address. Nor was there any disappointment. The relation was full and clear and positive. God had come to him by his special grace in the far-off land of his birth, and as he was passing over the great waters to his mother's home, and had wrought effectually in his conscience and his heart, making him feel that he was under a terrible condemnation; that the piety of ten thousand fathers and mothers could do him no good; that he could only be delivered and saved through the atoning blood of Jesus Christ, and by the mighty power of the Holy Spirit. He had bowed in humble submission, and the peace of God, which passeth all understanding, had filled his heart. He had consecrated his whole life to the service of his Redeemer, and was pressing onward in a course of thorough training for the Christian ministry, that he might go back and preach the glorious gospel in that dark land where his mother's zeal for Christ was consuming her last energies, and where she was soon to find a grave.

"No one saw, on that day of his public profession, the dark and terrible cloud which was rising over our beloved country, and under whose still deepening shadows the precious name of James Schneider was to be written on that long and mournful list of young, brave, Christian hearts so nobly sacrificed on the altar of liberty. To that deeply interested congregation, and, doubtless, to God, who accepts the purpose of the heart, that solemn act was the consecration of himself to Christ and the church as a faithful missionary of the cross to the heathen."

It may be added, as not without interest in connection with this sacred transaction, that, when the communion failed on the first Sabbath in January, for reasons above stated, young Schneider was persuaded to remain during the week at Framingham, with the expectation that the communion-service would certainly occur on the next Sabbath; though he felt sensitive about doing so, as it was term-time at Andover. But, when the communion-service again failed, he went back to Andover, and made another journey to Framingham, to be present on the first Sabbath in February.

This was in 1856. About one month from this time, Dr. Schneider started from Aintab to make his long looked-for and longed-for visit to this country, after an absence of twenty-two years, bringing back with him William, and leaving Eddie again to spend his days alone with his mother as he had before done with his father. Mrs. S. again had the offer of coming home; but as her visit had been so recently made, and such pressing duties and cares, of a public nature, called for her presence at Aintab, she, of her own free will, decided to remain and superintend the work during her husband's absence. Dr. Schneider reached this country in due course; and not far from the time he set foot upon his native shore, as afterwards appeared, Mrs. S. sickened and died of one of the malignant fevers of the East, leaving Eddie, now ten years old, without father or mother, brother or sister. Trouble of no ordinary character had come suddenly upon this little, scattered household, hitherto unbroken by death. Eddie, though alone, was not alone. The Christian Armenians hovered around him with their sympathy and care. Other missionaries were near. But it was thought best that he should go to Constantinople, and be in the family of Dr. Dwight until his father's return, and this plan was carried out. So matters stood in the fall of 1856.

CHAPTER V.

COLLEGE LIFE.

IN 1856, young Schneider finished his course at Phillips Academy and entered Yale College at the age of seventeen. His father reached this country, as already intimated, not long before, and rejoiced greatly at what he saw and heard of James. The quiet and modest lad with whom he had parted at Aintab, four years before, had grown into the form and proportions of a young man of pure and excellent character and fine promise, both intellectually and spiritually. Wherever he had lived, he had left behind him warm and earnest friends, and now he was passing on to the larger theatre of a college life. The faithful missionary, returning to his home after so many years' absence, and seeing how kindly his children were cared for, — his daughters at New Haven, and his son now to take up his residence there under most favorable auspices, had occasion to feel that God was truly faithful to his promise, " I will be a God to thee, and to thy seed after thee."

It was not until a month or more after his landing that the sad news from Aintab could reach Dr. S. in this country. It was a heavy blow to him and the four children here, who remembered their mother's prayers and counsels with devout affection and gratitude.

It had been the original intention at Aintab, so far as any definite plan had been formed, that James should be educated at Amherst College, as involving less expense and as being his father's *alma mater*. But the presence of his sisters at New Haven and Mr. Northrop's partialities for Yale college had combined to make an argument in favor of the latter institution, and Dr. S. had consented that his son should be educated there.

James's class, at the time of the issue of the first catalogue, numbered a hundred and thirty-four,—a large class, and yet not so large as several that had preceded it at different times, or as some that have since followed. His class at graduation numbered one hundred and eight, preserving its numbers better than classes at Yale usually do.

This relation of the final or graduating number to the entering number, in the various classes passing through Yale or other colleges, is a somewhat interesting subject for study. In the class of 1839, at Yale, the number on entrance was larger than in any previous year, — one hundred and thirty-five; but the class graduated only ninety-three. In the class of 1858, the entering number was one hundred and thirty-seven, and the graduating number just one hundred. The class of 1864 entered with one hundred and fifty-four, and graduated but one hundred and nine. This, however, was in the time of the war, and that, doubtless, made a difference. It is seldom that a class keeps the graduating number nearer to the entering number than did the class of 1860, of which Schneider was a member, — indicating that the stable elements were present in as large a degree, certainly, as usual.

The number given on the first catalogue after entrance is almost always likely to be greater than at any other point in the history of the class; but it does by no means include all the persons who will be numbered with the class in its progress through the institution. It almost always happens that individuals come dropping in through the whole of freshman year, who, by reason of sickness or for other causes, could not be present at the opening of the course. Then, at the beginning of sophomore year, quite a number, — sometimes ten, fifteen, or twenty, — who have been preparing themselves for that year, preferring to pursue the freshman studies elsewhere, come in in a body; and, on through sophomore, and even junior, year, there will still be additions, one by one. It is no uncommon thing at Yale for a class, that has had on its list during its course two hundred different students, to graduate not more than one hundred. Generally, the graduating number is not very much more than one half the whole number that have had some connection with the class at some stage in its history.

The causes operating to thin a class down after this manner are many and various, — ill-health; irregular habits, bringing the students under discipline, and at length suspension from college; want of mental capacity or application, so that the student falls below the necessary mark in scholarship; changes in the condition of parents, by which supplies have to be cut off, etc., etc. A boy who is poor, and who has in a large measure to engineer his own way, is about as apt to go through as any one. His habits are likely to be more regular and systematic. He has a great purpose from the start, and this steadies him. If a rich father happens to fail or die, his son in college, as he has not been trained to rely upon himself, will very likely have to abandon his course of study. But the poor boy (blessed be nothing!) has no one to upset his plans by failing or dying. He rests back upon the everlasting rock of poverty as his unfailing support.

The history of young men here in New England (and they are to be numbered by thousands) who have gone through our colleges without knowing afterward how they ever found their way through, sometimes gets written out, but more often goes into the silent and unwritten records of the past. But hope and courage are strong in young hearts, and they are not daunted by difficulties such as would utterly block the path of the timid and irresolute. Besides, it is ever a pleasing sight, when a young man of pure character and acting for noble ends is seen encountering such obstacles and manfully endeavoring to overcome them; and there are almost always kind and generous hearts that are moved with sympathy, and lend a helping hand,—a little here and a little there. Almost all our foreign missionaries and thousands of our ministers, living and dead, have been through their college course after this fashion.

Young Schneider entered Yale College on this principle of faith and trust. His father would do all that was in his power to do; but the small treasury at Aintab was not adequate for expenses like these. Some money must be borrowed, to be paid by teaching when his college course should be completed. Some money must be earned in such times and ways as Providence should open. The Education Society would gladly afford its measure of aid to the son, as it had done to the father before him, and kind friends would be raised up, who would help him lift and sustain the bur-

den. Through all these conspiring agencies
he went directly forward with his college
course, and soon came to take a stand among
the very first scholars in his class. Rev. Dr.
Dutton, whose house was near the college,
and was, as thousands can testify, the home
of open and generous hospitality, for a year
gave him his board. Others helped in various
ways. And so the hills of difficulty were
brought low, and the rough places were made
smooth before him, and he went on his way
joyfully, with all the glow and ardor of the
genuine student. For him, as for thousands
before him, his college life was eminently
happy. He rejoiced in it and was glad.
Here he was forming companionships which
only death could sunder. Here he was laying
broad and deep the foundation for a life of
extended usefulness. As a student, he bore
himself well, maintaining a very high rank
from the beginning to the end of his course.
As a Christian, he bore himself well, and
found a large field for activity. He was here
during the great revival in the winter of
1857–8, when the college was so powerfully
shaken, and which resulted in making a larger

proportion of the under-graduate students in the institution professors of religion than at any time before or since for a long course of years.

At the time when James's sisters, Susan and Eliza, were placed at school with Miss Dutton, in New Haven, it so happened that the two sons of Rev. H. G. O. Dwight, D. D. (so honorably known for his long and able missionary service at Constantinople, and so lamented when called away suddenly by death), were in this country for the purposes of education. The elder of the two, James H. Dwight, had graduated the very summer when these daughters of Dr. Schneider reached the country, and immediately commenced his theological course at Union Theological Seminary, where he graduated in 1855. The younger, William B. Dwight, was at that time a member of the junior class in Yale, graduating in course in 1854. He then pursued his theological studies at New York, graduating from Union Seminary in 1857. The children that had played familiarly together in Turkey were now, after several years of separation, brought together again in this land of their fathers. It was but natural, from all the rich and precious associations of the past, that, meeting thus, far away from their early home, they should be deeply interested in each other. That might have been, and there it might have ended. But it was destined to be otherwise. The renewed acquaintance and friendship ripened into a deeper affection, and, in the course of a few years, Susan Schneider became the wife of James H. Dwight, and Eliza Schneider the wife of William B. Dwight.

In novels, things are made often to adjust themselves as nicely and harmoniously as this; but they seldom do in real life. Every one felt that there was something beautiful in such an arrangement. Parents and friends and outside observers all felt like breathing a blessing upon so happy a union. A short time after their marriage, their residence was at Englewood, New Jersey, where Rev. James H. Dwight was, and still is, the pastor of the Presbyterian Church, and Rev. W. B. Dwight was for some years at the head of a school. We shall find, in the later parts of our narrative, that many things date from Englewood, and the above will explain the reason of this.

We will presently give a few extracts from the letters of James, written during this period, which will help in some measure to unfold his thoughts and feelings during his life at New Haven; though we have in our possession comparatively few of his college-day epistles. We have abundant materials of this kind illustrative of the years that passed after he left college, and, as the interest of his life so concentrates about this later period, we can afford to pass somewhat rapidly over these college years, which, though filled with that which intensely occupied his time and his thought, were not materially unlike those of other earnest, faithful, Christian students passing through the same course of study. He very much endeared himself to his instructors, to his fellow-students, and to all about him. He was in vigorous health, and able to endure the labor and confinement of the course without injury. He came to the end of his college course ranking, notwithstanding all the disadvantages of his early life, as the third scholar in a class of one hundred and eight.

It was during his college course that his father went back to Aintab. He remained in this country two years, most usefully employed in laboring among the churches and in visits to various religious bodies, both in New England, in the Middle States, and at the West. In this way he helped to diffuse abroad valuable missionary intelligence respecting the work of God in the Turkish Empire, and thus increase the missionary spirit of the churches. He returned to his home in the East in the fall of 1858, when James was entering upon his junior year. A short time before his departure, he was united in marriage to Miss Susan M. Abbott, the youngest sister of his former wife, who, by her education and earnest Christian character, was well fitted for the high and honorable position to which she was chosen. The only circumstance which made this decision painful to her was the fact that she must leave her mother, — a widow far advanced in life, and to whom she had been for many years a constant companion and helper, and especially so, since her father's death, which occurred only a few years before. This made the question a trying one. But as other members of the family were willing to assume this responsibility and care, and as the judgment of her Christian friends strongly seconded her own desire to go, she went; but with the understanding that she should return, at no distant date, to visit her mother, if she lived, and comfort her declining days.

Dr. S. returned to the scene of his labors, with the feeling that the four children left behind in this country were all passing on to stations of honor and usefulness.

In his vacations James was naturally much at Framingham; and the impressions he was there making upon people may be gathered from a brief extract from a letter which went from Framingham to Dr. Dutton in New Haven. The following is the passage referred to: — " In the few lines which I wrote you the other day, I forgot to mention, what I had intended, how much our people were pleased, last Sunday evening, with some remarks which James Schneider made in our meeting, and with the prayer which he offered. . . . . It was a very large meeting for us, and Schneider's remarks were so quiet and gentle, and at the same time so full of feeling, and so much to the point, that people listened with breathless attention. The house was very still. I think he is going to make an admirable man."

His brother William,* who had returned with Dr. S. to this country, was at this time at Williston Academy, Easthampton, and there he, too, as he hoped and believed, had experienced the renewing grace of God upon his heart, and was passing on successfully in his course of education.

It was during the month of February, 1860, the last year of James's college life, that his eldest sister, Susan, wife of Rev. James H. Dwight, was called away. It was the first break in the circle of the children, and was a sad affliction to the whole household. His

---

* We shall not attempt to trace minutely the life of this brother, and yet, for the sake of giving clearness to our narrative, it is needful to state, that, after finishing his studies at Easthampton and Andover, he went to Washington to be employed in the hospitals of that city. Here he was taken sick, and brought near the borders of the grave. After a long illness and a slow recovery, he studied engineering, and in September, 1863, became third assistant engineer on board the war-vessel Calypso. He was afterwards promoted to be second assistant, and still later was transferred to the Roanoke, where he remained until after the close of the war. In the summer of 1865, he resigned, and is now fitting himself for the business of mining engineering.

sister Eliza (Mrs. E. H. Dwight), in a recent letter, says: — "Susie died February 13, 1860. Her death made a very strong impression upon James. His great and loving heart was stirred to its very depths; and from that time his piety was of a higher order, and his advancement in the Christian course marked and progressive."

In order to show what was passing in his thoughts during his college life, we will now cull, from his letters written at that period, a few brief extracts. It will be seen by these varied expressions, uttered in perfect freedom to his sisters, that, while he was an earnest and growing Christian, he was by no means an ascetic, but had in him, in large measure, the sport and play of youth. We will not attempt to fix exact dates to these passages, but will give them somewhat at random, as illustrative of the operations of his mind from 1856 to 1860. The extracts are taken from letters sent to his two sisters, sometimes to one, and sometimes the other, until after Susan's death, and to Eliza when she was left alone. In one of these letters he says: — "Tremendous excitement in town to-night! The last campaign speeches have been made, — the last public lie told, — the last appeal addressed to the conscience (if she has any) of Connecticut. We of college are interested; some of us are even made voters. I am a *voter;* and if I don't cast my vote for Buckingham, with pride and indignation commingled, then I am not myself."

In one of his college vacations, he went out with some other religious students, gathering facts as to the religious condition of the towns in Connecticut. These young men were in the service of the General Association of the State. He had heard that the region assigned to him was rather unattractive for this kind of labor. He writes: —
"This county (where he was going), they say, is rough, and the people hard and heathenish. But a fellow that's been in Aintab, and had stones whizzing by his ears, can probably endure considerable in the way of rough treatment."

He is desirous of making a certain journey for pleasure, in one of his vacations; but he has to reason the case to his sisters to justify himself, in the matter of expense. "But let us consider the matter. I have been in college nearly three years. All that while I am not conscious of a single extravagance. Shall I not be allowed a little freedom now? I know little of mankind in general, and womankind in particular. I shall soon be out in the world. Ought I not to be acquainted with its ways? Don't I need to go into society; and will not an excursion into the midst of strangers, and yet refined people, be beneficial? Even in this utilitarian point of view, it seems to me that this proposed visit presents attractions that are worthy of consideration."

To Eliza he writes:—"I was greatly rejoiced to get your letter. I had been longing to have even a word from you, but hardly dared to hope for a note, knowing how busy you were. So I contented myself with picturing in imagination, how you looked, and what you were doing,—Charley* now yawning, now stretching, now taking music-lessons, now performing optical experiments in estimating magnitudes and dis-

---

* The little child, here and elsewhere spoken of, is the dear babe, left by his sister Susan, when six or seven days old, and now kindly adopted and cared for by Eliza.

tances, now given to the bottle and clinging to it as the staff of life. Oh, the dear little chick! wouldn't I like to kiss him? . . . . The precious little sage has doubtless brains enough in that capacious head of his to build a Turkish republic out of; but he wisely remains *incog.* at present. . . . . I need hardly tell you that the reality and greatness of our loss (in Susie's death) are becoming daily more apparent; and weighty sorrow sinks deeper and deeper into my heart. Scarcely an hour passes but I think of dear Susie, and countless objects and incidents bring her before my mind. Her memory I cherish with growing attachment and respect. God and heaven are much nearer to me now, and a different light seems to be cast over the world. I am far happier than I have been and far sadder, too, — happy when I think of the joys of heaven, and of meeting mother and sister there, and sad when I revert to our bereavement."

Again he writes on the same topic : — " Last Sunday I read some of Susie's letters. Oh, what a dear, loving sister there was! Every line bears the record of her overflowing love.

I never felt her loss as I do now, but I did not like to tell you of my grief, because I knew you had enough of sorrow. Study takes up my attention; but when I get a moment to think, my thoughts fly to the single grave at Englewood. Can it be that Susie lies there? I hope to kneel beside it in a few weeks. . . . . . Wont you save something of Susie's for me as a memento; also a lock of her hair?"

His commencement is drawing nigh, and he writes to his sister: — " Are you coming? For your own sake I should be delighted to have you come, and you would certainly be benefited by the trip; but if you are coming solely on my account, I will readily excuse you. My piece is a dry metaphysical production, and probably will not be understood, even if listened to, by more than fifty people in the house. It is my first attempt at genuine public speaking, and I very much fear you would be disappointed. It will be over, too, in twelve minutes or so. How dear Susie used to look forward to this time! Wont it be sad for you to come alone?"

We might multiply these extracts, but must

forbear. They are taken simply from his letters to his sisters, because we have not access to letters written elsewhere during this period.

CHAPTER VI.

HIS CONNECTION WITH THE NORMAL SCHOOL AT BRIDGEWATER.

WHEN young Schneider had completed his college course, it was necessary for him, before studying theology, to engage for a time in teaching, that he might cancel the debts incurred by his education, assist his brothers, and obtain the means of finishing his own course of study. Fortunately, Rev. Mr. Northrop, connected as he was with the State Board of Education in Massachusetts, had it, in a measure, entrusted to his care to fill a vacant place in the Bridgewater State Normal School, and in his judgment, and in the judgment of others having knowledge of the facts, Schneider was just the man to fill it. The result abundantly justified this opinion. He writes from Saxonville, to his sister, Saturday evening, September 8, 1860: —

"DEAR LIZZIE, — Hereafter you will please to address me as First Assistant Principal of the State Normal School at Bridgewater. Are not my wildest hopes realized now? . . . . This is another blessing. My college life was prospered by Heaven, and now my entrance into life is brightened by a new benignity. I am right happy to-night. Do you think it strange? Suspense is not very pleasant. This position is just what I wanted, — one involving not generalship but study. I enter upon my duties upon the 19th, and meanwhile shall be getting ready. . . . . Good-night. A happy and peaceful Sabbath to you.
"Ever yours,
"JAMES."

With his habit of doing everything thoroughly, so soon as he had received this appointment, and before entering upon its duties, he spent the interval in daily attendance upon the Normal School at Framingham, and in a visit to the one at Salem, that he might study the methods and modes of instruction in such institutions, and be prepared to enter upon his work intelligently. He was to receive a salary of nine hundred dollars a year for his services; and to a young man, who has been struggling with poverty all the way through college, the thought of such an income lifts a great burden from the soul. Alluding to some help, which had come just before from an unexpected quarter, he says:—" What could be more fortunate than Mr. Kelker's generosity! Oh, how glad I am! Now Willie and I can get along nicely till the end of the term, and then I hope to have some money that I myself have earned." He says again:—" Next Monday I go to Bridgewater. Now once more for hard work. This year I expect will be far more busy than any I have yet lived, and I hope you will see some improvement in your brother, as the result. I cannot help thinking myself highly fortunate in getting such a position."

He entered upon his work, at Bridgewater, with thankfulness in his heart toward God, who had so kindly watched over and provided for him thus far, and, with a deep and solemn purpose to do his duty. After he had been sometime engaged in his work there, he writes to his sister: — "These have been weeks of intense but happy work, and I find myself in a peculiarly happy frame of mind this morning."

We have reached a point in his history, where we have it far more in our power, than in the previous parts of the narrative, to illustrate his life and modes of thought and feeling from his own letters, and we propose in this chapter to make free use of this material. But as dates, in such a connection, are of comparatively little value to the reader, we shall, except in special instances, omit them.

Alluding to the work to which he had now set his hands, he says: — "We are to have a full school and plenty of work. . . . . I feel most uncomfortably sometimes at the thought of the responsibility resting upon me. May God keep me from giving a defective form to the education of any of these minds."

Again: — "There is no end to the skill to be exercised in bringing out the energies of the variously constituted minds in the school.

The best test of the teacher is his success in stirring up the dull scholar."

In the fall of 1861 he writes: — "One thing troubles me. I have been at Bridgewater till I have much improved, and can now teach five times as well as at the outset. And it seems that the school ought to have the advantage of this tuition, which it has itself bestowed. And then having begun to be a teacher, I don't like to stop till I am a proficient in it. But my plan is to study theology next year. How and when, God will direct."

Again he says: — "I begin to wish that I were in my life-work. I don't want to keep breaking up old associations. Unconsciously we become attached to places and people; and man does not relish being transplanted, any more than trees. To give your energies to one pursuit, and then change their direction, is not strengthening. It is very hard for me to make up my mind, though I am resolved to begin the study of theology, unless a different course is plainly pointed out. I want much to make a fine scholar. I think I lack a practical turn of mind. I am much attached to this place, and to leave it will cost an effort;

but I can do it. We are very much what circumstances make us. How good God has been to me in this regard! What might I not have been, thrown as I was upon myself, in a new world? Why have I been so securely protected from temptation?"

His religious life was greatly quickened here at Bridgewater. From various expressions in his letters, some of which have been quoted, it was evident, about the time of his leaving college, and for quite a period afterwards, that he felt the stirrings of earthly ambition, and was greatly tempted to abandon the plans of his earlier days, and give himself to scholarship. But he is coming now again to higher and nobler views of life, as the two following extracts from letters will show: —

"Last night we had a joyful prayer-meeting. It was the last of the term, and gratitude to God, for the precious hours we have spent in that room, filled all our hearts. I am very glad we did not give them up when our numbers were so small. They have done us much good, and resulted in one or two conversions. Two weeks ago, God seemed to hide himself, and though I prayed, I did not seem to have access to him. Now he comes to me again, and I am happy. We all have such experiences, I think."

April 27, 1862, he writes as follows. We give this date as marking an important era in his religious experience, and in the purpose of his life.

"The conflict is over, and the question is decided. I am resolved, by God's help, to be a minister, and that, too, a missionary. I have, on my knees and with tears, thus given myself to God. This is my resolution, and I shall adhere to it, unless future events plainly point to some other path. I have reasoned thus about the matter. First, what is the principle upon which I am to decide the question? Of course my object is to be, to do good. How, then, can I do the greatest good? As a missionary? Yes, I think so. For this reason: I am fond of study and thought; but if I give myself up to some work which will admit of this, and stay in this country, my ambition will, I am afraid, carry me away, and I may become a selfish, useless man. But if I am a missionary, ambition is at once crushed out. But what if the work be really and naturally distasteful? No, it shall not be, if prayer can prevent it. God, I hope, will give me grace. And do you think he will so order events as to thwart my most natural desires and tastes? No; he will not let me suffer in that way. I can trust him. He may be in this way trying my faith. I will give myself to this humble work, expecting nothing, aiming at nothing more. And if God, in his providence, finds work for me other than this, I will gladly accept it. . . . . This, I say, is my decision. I see no reason to change it. I have written to Mr. Northrop, asking his advice, and await his answer. But I think he will advise this course. What my immediate duty to my brothers may be is a question. Eddie is coming over. It may be necessary for me to work for them longer. I will cheerfully do it, if it is my duty, though I wish to be at my life-work. God will direct. I am feeling better, much calmer, happier."

In his own thought, at the time he formed the full purpose to become a missionary, it was apparently settled that this decision would involve his retirement from Bridgewater, in order that he might enter at once upon the study of theology. He had, however, an afterthought, that his duty to his brothers, and especially to Eddie, who was coming over to be educated, might require him to defer for a season the commencement of his theological studies. On conversing with his Christian friends upon this point, while they heartily approved his purpose to become a missionary, they thought, both for his brothers' sake and for other reasons, he might remain awhile longer at Bridgewater. He was very useful there. He was greatly beloved both by his fellow-teachers and by the pupils. He was exerting a happy Christian influence upon many minds. The Spirit of God was in the institution, and souls were converted. For all these reasons he decided to remain.

When he communicated his purpose to become a missionary, to his father, there came back from Aintab the following glad response. The letter is dated July 30th, 1862:—

"Another source of joy to us was your decision to become a missionary. It was what I had all the time desired; but I wished you to make the decision from your own interest in the subject, and not by my arguments. I do rejoice that you have come to this determination, and that you seem to be so happy in it. This very fact seems to show that you have taken the proper course. I have no doubt that you will be quite as happy, if not more so, in the missionary field, than you would be in America. I have no doubt that I have experienced more real satisfaction in my work than I should have realized in America. And then you will, with God's blessing, be instrumental of more good. You will find an abundance of scope for all the talents and acquirements you possess. In translating books, or teaching in some of our seminaries, your scholarship will all be called into requisition, should you be introduced into this sphere. No kind of talents and no degree of attainments come amiss. I have often wished I knew *everything*, and had all history at my command, both sacred and profane; there are times when all comes into play. And then a knowledge of the physical sciences is often very desirable, *in all their minutiæ*. A taste and tact for language is, of course, very important to the missionary. I think you love the languages. That is well. Cultivate that taste.

But you need not be anxious on the point of how you may employ your attainments. Acquire all the knowledge you can, and commit your ways to the Lord, and he will direct you into the right path. And when you are ready to come out to this country, be assured you will receive from us a most hearty welcome. The Lord order it all in great mercy. I have no doubt that He will do so."

But amid all his thoughts and plans there is another subject which begins to press home upon his conscience and heart.

In a letter, bearing date Aug. 5th, 1862, he says: — "I feel much about the war. I almost want to volunteer. I want to do some good, and there are so many noble fellows that are giving themselves up, that I want to be among them. One of my classmates, a fine fellow, died in the hospital the other day. I am liable to be drafted at Bridgewater. Duty! let me do my duty."

In the August following he says: — "These late fearful battles! How many afflicted and cast down now! O God, have mercy, and forgive! My heart aches for these bereaved and suffering ones. What can I do for them? Is this a time to be anything else than a man?" And again:—"I am feeling really sober to-night. In the first place, this war troubles me. I begin to think the nation is in a bad way, and needs my attention. I have thought of this matter seriously, and do not consider it my duty to go at present. There may come a time when there will be a more urgent demand, and then I may feel it my duty to go. Still the question comes up."

His brother Edward has now reached this country, and the sense of duty toward him has much to do in making him feel that the time has not yet come for him to join the army. He felt greatly the responsibility thrown upon him, in the care of this young brother, who as yet had enjoyed very few advantages of education, and was moreover impulsive in his temperament and liable to be easily led astray. Edward was placed in a school at Bridgewater, that he might be near his brother, and enjoy his oversight and assistance.

In the month of October James writes:—
"Eddie, I think, may be a comfort to me, instead of a burden. He is affectionate and grateful, and bright when he has a mind to study."

In the midst of all his other cares and duties, as his letters show, he is engaged in solid reading, that he may store his mind with the higher thoughts of the race.

"I have read about Bacon lately, and am wishing for a little of his wisdom and wealth of thought. I have been waiting a long time for some grand, inspiring thought to come to me, but it does not make its appearance. I think I cannot be a genius. I had no thought, at Phillips Academy, of overturning the Hamiltonian system of Philosophy, as Bacon did of subverting the Aristotelian system of Logic, when at Cambridge. But, episodically, I have just found a book which I have long wanted, and that written, too, by Bacon."

The following extracts, too, will show the current of his thought: —

"What a delight it must be to watch the unfolding of a mind! As much as it is to watch a budding plant. What are we? What mysteries! I wonder how we shall look upon each other and ourselves in another state. Shall we laugh at our notions of this lower state? You know how one feels, when, after working at a problem, and solving it, as he supposes, he finds himself entirely mistaken, and foolishly mistaken. Poor philosophers! What a shock to their sensitive natures the revelations of the next world will prove!

"I am in Mr. Boyden's study this evening. He and his wife have gone to attend the funeral services of a cousin, who died in one of the recent battles, and they wished me to come and stay with the boys. Oh this war! How dreadful! It makes one sick. I want to go and do something. I'm afraid I am too selfish, though I try not to be. But I feel very sober and earnest. I mean to be industrious, and do all that is in my power. This is no time for self-indulgence. I do wish to have some part in this great war, — this grand era of history. To look on as a spectator seems very belittling. But I must be patient, and work in my humble sphere.

"You notice what father says about my studying. I think that nothing that I acquire here will come amiss. Then there will be so much satisfaction in having a well-rounded education. Surely, are we not preparing for heaven by cultivating our minds?

"I feel very happy. I think I am doing my duty. I love God more, I hope. I love my scholars and my work, and I love the heathen and my coming work. My mind and heart can expand together. To-day I shall get a harmony of the Gospels by Robinson. I want to study the life of Christ."

Eddie, who, he thought might prove a comfort to him rather than a burden, in the early months of his stay at Bridgewater, was really a heavy care and responsibility, and James had many anxious thoughts respecting him. He was impulsive; was perpetually restless, with a longing to be old enough to join the army; had not yet learned how to study; so that from the time of his arrival, on through the winter of 1862–3, he added largely to his brother's burden. But James labored with him faithfully and bore with him patiently, and soon had the satisfaction of seeing a better day dawning. In the spring and early summer of 1863, there was a revival in Bridgewater, which took hold of the young people gathered there for study, as also of the community at large, and, on June 9th, James writes to a friend: —

"Eddie is most thoroughly under conviction. I talked with him when we were walking together. I may have done wrong. I told him that, in order to become a Christian, he must be willing to give up everything to Christ, — that he must even give up the army. It brought him into a fierce struggle. He said he would give up everything but the army. He says he wants to give up even that, but that it is very hard, and he cannot do it yet. He became most morbidly depressed in feeling, and wished himself dead. He feels happier this morning, and is going to the prayer-meeting, and may take part in it, in discharge of duty. Not only pray for him, but write to him, please. *Noon.* — Eddie is feeling much better. We went to the prayer-meeting, but there was no meeting, no notice having been given out. He is willing to do his duty I think. I am quite confident he will be a Christian. Can we be thankful enough? I am very happy to-day; conscious of weakness, and yet strong."

Two days later he writes: — " I'm so happy in Eddie. I really think he is a Christian. He seems a new boy. He was never so gentle, obliging, courteous as now. He seems to be willing to do anything that God shall require of him."

But we must turn back for a moment to something which belongs to an earlier date.

As already stated, when Mrs. Schneider went out to Aintab, in 1858, leaving her aged mother behind, it was with the understanding and pledge that she should return for a visit at no distant date. The time has passed quickly in our narrative, but nearly five years have gone since she left the country. About the middle of May, 1863, she landed in Boston. James hears of it at Bridgewater, and writes at once: — "My precious mother, I want to fly to you. . . . . Happily my vacation commences next Friday night." But hardly had she reached the country and taken a hasty glance at her New England friends, when a message reached her from Carbondale, Pa., which called her thither at once. Her mother was living there with a grandson, Rev. Benjamin H. Abbott, the Episcopal minister of the place. He and his sister residing with him had gratefully remembered the kindness and care shown them, in their own early life, when left orphans in the world, and they had kindly invited their grandmother, in the weakness and feebleness of her old age, to make her home with them. She had met with a fall, which had seriously injured her. This happened almost at the very time when Mrs. S. set foot upon our shores, and hence the sudden message calling her thither, where she remained until her mother's death, about the first of August.

Eddie's conversion, it will be remembered, was after Mrs. S. landed and went to Carbondale. On the 20th of June, James writes her: — "What will you say and think when you hear that Eddie is a Christian? It is God's doing, and it is marvellous in our eyes. I think he is sincere, and that he is truly converted. You would think so had you seen the struggle which preceded it. He did not want to give up the army; but I told him, unless he was willing to give up the army, *in case God demanded it of him*, he could not be a Christian. It was almost too much for him; but he finally submitted, and is now at peace. I hope so, at least. I tremble sometimes, however. Pray, pray for him. My heart's best love to dear good grandmother; tell her I wish I could do something to contribute to her comfort."

In his letters to Mrs. S. he usually addresses her, as "My dear Auntie." In one of his letters he says:—"I am going to call you so, when I speak to you by yourself; but before others I will call you mother; otherwise they will think it strange. Auntie is a much dearer name when I speak to you, and my love to you flows much more readily through that name. Now you do not misunderstand me,—do you?"

But now, for many months, this war question has been seriously troubling him. He cannot quite decide, under all the circumstances of the case, and against the wishes of friends, that it is his duty to go, and yet he stands in doubt, and wishes to do his duty. And now the time draws near for a decision. He is about to close his third year at Bridgewater, and does not intend to return. If he does not go into the army, he will enter upon his theological course. Moreover, a draft is coming, and he is disposed to take that decision as an expression of the will of God on the great question at issue. July 11th he writes:—"The draft in this town comes off next Monday. I stand one fourth of a chance. What shall I do if I am called? Shall I go? I think I shall. It will seem like a call from God. . . . It will not do for every man to stay away. . . . Will any one say that the principles at stake are not worth fighting for, or that his life is too valuable when put beside them? The war may continue many years. I may never come back. O God, show me the way. Help me to feel my duty. . . Make me do thy will. So I rest."

At the close of a letter, written July 19th, he says: — "I shall keep this open till about the time the mail closes, so as to tell you, if possible, whether I am called or not."

" [*Postscript.*] I am called. God wills it."

CHAPTER VII.

ENTERS THE ARMY. ORDAINED AND BECOMES CHAPLAIN.

THE year of the school, at Bridgewater, closed not far from the time when young Schneider was drafted, making the full period of his connection with that institution just three school years.

The step he was now taking was a momentous one, and he so regarded it. It was no hasty and ill-considered decision. He had pondered over this subject for months,—had struggled with it, as all his letters abundantly show; and in coming to the conclusion which he had now reached, never did a young man bow more reverently and obediently to the sense of duty, to the voice of conscience, against all the siren whispers of ease and pleasure and self-gratification. It was his profound conviction that duty summoned him, and he must go.

Indeed, it is rare, that a young man is called to make such a decision, with so many influences tending to hold him back. There was one, now dear to him as his own life, to whom he was betrothed, and who looked forward with him to a missionary life in Turkey, not as something to be shunned if possible, but to be sought with eager Christian joy. He loved her with all the strength of a pure, uncontaminated soul in the fresh ardors of youth. That love was too strong and too honest to be concealed. It comes out, as from a pent-up fountain, in all his familiar letters to his near friends.

Then, just at this time, he received an appointment to a tutorship in Yale College, — a place which, under other circumstances, he would most joyfully have accepted. Nothing, seemingly, could have been more fortunate for him, just at this time, than to have gone back to Yale in this capacity, where he would have been brought into associations tending to a large general culture, — would have been able to pursue his theological studies, and have been on pay as a tutor at the same time. It was a sore trial to say No, to an offer at once so honorable, so pleasing, and so convenient.

Then he knew the wishes and hopes of all his near friends. He knew how patiently and longingly his father, honored and beloved, was waiting for the day when this dear son should come back to Turkey, to be associated with himself in missionary work.

All these things are to be considered as powerful motives additional to the natural repugnance which a studious and highly cultivated mind like his would feel to the rough and boisterous associations of the camp. For, be it remembered, when he makes this great decision, it is not with any definite military office or honor in prospect. He is drafted as a common soldier, and it is with the lot of a common soldier in view, that he adds that brief postscript, "I am called. God wills it."

From Valatie, New York, where he is visiting at the house of his uncle, Alexander Abbott, he writes to his father: —

"MY DEAR FATHER, — You have long looked for this letter. You have heard that I go to the war, and wish to know my reasons for a change of plan so complete as this. In the first place, then, I do not go to the war because I have lost my interest in the missionary work. On the contrary, I love that work more strongly and naturally, and anticipate it with enthusiasm. . . .

"I *do* go to the war, because, first, I was *drafted*. The lot fell upon me. God, who marks the sparrow's fall, guides the slip of paper that falls from the revolving wheel. I am *called*. This is not a sufficient reason, but then it throws the burden of proof on *me*. Secondly, our army needs men of intelligence, but, above all, of moral principle. There are not men enough in the army of such character. The good that such men can do in the army is incalculable, and not second in importance to the missionary work. Lastly, I made the question a subject of prayer, and tried to decide conscientiously. I feel now that I did decide as my conscience dictated. I had the assurance that I was doing right. It was the most painful question that I have ever debated. Whichever way I should decide would involve hardship and trouble. I have given myself up to the work. I shall try to live usefully, and if I am called to die, I shall die cheerfully. . . . . Your affectionate son,

"JAMES."

Surely here is a decision that must win the respect of all serious and thoughtful minds. Such calm obedience to the simple idea of duty, when so many influences appear to turn the heart aside, is noble and heroic anywhere.

Not very far from the same time, he writes from Saxonville:— "I had a good talk with Aunt Susie (his mother) this morning. She does not think I ought to go. But it is only because she loves me, and can't part with me, that she talks so. It is painful not to have the cordial support of all my friends; and still I feel that I am in the right." * Again, he says:— "When I listen to the dissuasions of my friends, I hear, way down in my heart, a voice which says,— Be resolute. You are right. God will shield you." In a letter to Mrs. S. he says:— "My precious, dear Auntie, shall I forfeit your priceless love by going to the war? I am sure I do not go from false motives.

* It may be mentioned here that after these talks with James, Mrs. S., in conversation with her friends, used to say, that she could but be astonished when she saw such perfect consecration on James's part to the idea of duty. There seemed then to be such a ripeness for heaven, that she could not but tremble through fear of his early departure from earthly scenes.

I shall try to do good, whatever may be my work. I think God has given me this work." In another letter, about this time, we find the following: — " It is not my pride that leads me, I know. It is a sense of duty. I am right and thank God. If I am wrong, God forgive me; I intend no wrong."

On hearing of his grandmother's death at Carbondale, he writes to his mother: — " God has been indeed very gracious to us in sparing dear grandmother until you returned, and so were able to minister to her comfort and consolation. How peaceful and sweet was her death! How rapidly is our family in heaven increasing! Edward, or I, or both may be there soon."

Nor far from the same time, he writes again: — " I have sad news to tell you. Dear little Willie, Eliza's birdie, has flown. He breathed his sweet life away this (Monday) morning at five o'clock."

He feels the painfulness of parting with dear A., and knows how sad it is for her; though she, too, with the same high sense of duty, will not complain, or seek to hinder. To his mother, he says, in the midst of this conflict of feeling : — " She is the most blessed gift, I was about to say, that God could bestow upon poor me. Oh, God is good." In another letter to his mother, he says: — " I hope we — A. and I — will be a great comfort to you and father." And in a letter to another: — " I cannot tell you how precious A. has become to me, — never so precious as now."

All this serves to remind us that there are those who stay at home, and yet suffer as keenly and exhibit as true a heroism as those who go. Thomas Buchanan Read, in his stanzas entitled " The Brave at Home," has beautifully and touchingly set forth this idea:

> " The maid who binds her warrior's sash
>   With smile that well her pain dissembles,
> The while beneath her drooping lash
>   One starry tear-drop hangs and trembles,
> Though Heaven alone records the tear,
>   And Fame shall never know her story,
> Her heart shall shed a drop as dear
>   As ever dewed the field of glory.

> " The wife who girds her husband's sword
>   Mid little ones who weep or wonder,
> And gravely speaks the cheering word,
>   What though her heart be rent asunder, —
> Doomed nightly in her dreams to hear
>   The bolts of war around him rattle, —
> Has shed as sacred blood as e'er
>   Was poured upon a field of battle.

"The mother who conceals her grief
  When to her breast her son she presses,
Then breathes a few brave words and brief,
  Kissing the patriot brow she blesses,
With no one but her secret God
  To know the pain that weighs upon her,
Sheds holy blood as e'er the sod
  Received on Freedom's field of honor."

As we have already said, at the time he was drafted he had no definite idea what his place or lot would be in the army, but by the suggestion of friends, his own impulses moving him in the same direction, he presented himself for examination at Washington, that he might be assigned to some place in connection with one of the colored regiments then forming. After the examination had passed, he writes to his mother: —

"WASHINGTON, Aug. 27, 1863.

"DEAR *Auntie* MOTHER, — I have passed examination, — a severe one, — and am appointed second lieutenant. I should have had a higher position had I known more of military. I now go home to study and await orders. I shall go up to Valatie for a few days. I am thankful and well pleased. In haste,

"Your own JAMIE boy."

He writes to another friend more fully about this examination : — "I was examined this morning, and did very well on the *civil* part, but had poor success in the *military* tactics. . . Gen. Casey (in private) expressed himself highly pleased with my 'scholarship,' advised me to go at once to studying, assuring me that I would soon be promoted. They examined me in Arithmetic, Algebra, Geometry, Trigonometry, Chemistry, History, Geography, and 'Casey.' I made them open their eyes when I was sent to the board. It was a little exciting, but it assures me that a thorough education never comes amiss. The examiners noticed the very points that we dwell on in the Normal school, — sharpness, accuracy. Any kind of knowledge does one much good in the struggles of life. I only value more highly all that I have acquired. . . I meet with men of great intelligence at times, and it is a rich treat to be in their company. Gen. Casey seems to be a well-informed man, and is very courteous withal."

At the time young Schneider entered the army, the process of forming colored regiments was going on vigorously. The 54th and 55th colored regiments from Massachusetts had gone out during the previous spring and summer,— the first *State* regiments of colored men which had been organized. But United States colored regiments were forming, and the 2d U. S. colored troops, was now nearly completed, and was encamped on Arlington Heights.

The colonel of this regiment was Stark Fellows, who graduated at Dartmouth College in 1862, and very soon after joined himself to the 14th regiment of New Hampshire volunteers, and held the office of first lieutenant in Co. D. In the fall of 1862, this regiment was ordered to Washington, and, during the winter and spring, Lieutenant Fellows, with a section of men under his command, was engaged in guard duty in the city. Here he attracted the favorable notice of public men, for his soldierly bearing, his promptness and efficiency in the performance of his duties, and for the strict order and decorum of the men under him. He gave himself, too, in all his leisure hours, most earnestly and assiduously to the study of military science and tactics, and in the summer of 1863 presented himself before the Board of Examiners, to try and obtain the office of

major, in some colored regiment. It was a
long step from first lieutenant to major, and
he feared that his proposal might be regarded
as somewhat audacious. But to his surprise,
after passing examination, he received a note,
from some one acting for the board, assuring
him that he had been too modest, and that
the office of colonel would be given him.

In the Adjutant General's report, New
Hampshire, Vol. II., p. 408, where the history
of the 14th N. H. regiment is given, this matter
is thus noticed : —

"Two officers of great excellence presented
themselves to Gen. Casey's board, in the summer
of 1863, for examination for commissions
in colored regiments. They were Major Samuel
A. Duncan and First Lieutenant Stark
Fellows. Both passed the board as colonel,
the first who had passed to that grade in a
number of hundreds examined, — and were
soon commissioned to new regiments, very
much regretted and respected in the regiment
they had left."

Col. Fellows was at this time but twenty-
three years of age. The instances were few, in
our army, where so young a man received so

high a command. But he was admirably fitted for his place. Of fine personal appearance, of pleasing address, with a manly and soldierly bearing, he knew how to win the love and respect of these humble colored men, yea, to bind them to himself as with hooks of steel. The attachment of the soldiers of the 2d U. S. colored regiment to their young colonel was extraordinary, and often spoken of in newspapers and private letters. The following passage, giving the substance of a portion of a lecture by Col. J. W. Higginson, who also commanded a colored regiment, the 1st South Carolina, will exhibit, in some measure, what Col. Fellows' thoughts and feelings and modes of action were in his new position, and will explain the philosophy by which he bound these men so closely to himself: - -

"As a preface to his address, Colonel Higginson explained that army life in a black regiment was not greatly unlike army life in a white regiment, and a black soldier did not differ very materially from a white soldier; yet they had their peculiarities, which were noticeable to the observer. He then spoke of the confusion of everything to him when he began the life; the perplexity he and his brother officers experienced in trying to distinguish individuals in the crowd of dusky faces,— to know Adam from Apollo, Sam from Pompey; and then, too, the trouble in learning the age of these men,— the world's eternal children, who never looked young or old: none of them had any idea of their age, and the enlisting officers were left to decide the matter by guesswork. Their qualities of heart, head, and hand were then considered by the speaker. It was with the heart that the officers first came in contact. The colored race are naturally demonstrative, and are like children; they feel towards their officers, if treated right, as the child towards the father. The liberties with superior officers that are repressed in the white soldier, because they lead to familiarities that are dangerous to discipline, are allowed in the black. The qualities needed to command a colored regiment are like those needed to command a white regiment,— energy, common sense and self-control; if he has these the work is essentially accomplished. Force or severe discipline should not be used so much as personal affection shown. These men, having been accustomed to severe treatment, are quickly influenced by kindness, sympathy, and respect. They will obey much quicker if appealed to than threatened."

This regiment, to which Schneider was assigned, already numbering about nine hundred men, was encamped on Arlington Heights. The whole formation of it had been under Col. Fellows' superintendence, and he had shaped it according to his own idea. It was something noble, at that time, for young men to step forward and put themselves into direct connection with these black men. There were many to sneer and laugh; but a crisis had been reached in our national affairs, and the nation has reason to rejoice that so many, in spite of all sneers and ridicule, were ready to discern the "signs of the times," and act promptly.

James Russell Lowell has well and beautifully said: —

" When a deed is done for Freedom, through the broad earth's aching breast
Runs a thrill of joy prophetic, trembling on from East to West;
And the slave, where'er he cowers, feels the soul within him climb.

To the awful verge of manhood, as the energy sublime
Of a century burst full-blossomed on the thorny stem of Time.
. . . .
"For mankind are one in spirit, and an instinct bears along,
Round the earth's electric circle, the swift flash of right or
   wrong;
Whether conscious or unconscious, yet humanity's vast
   frame,
Through its ocean-sundered fibres, feels the gush of joy or
   shame;
In the gain or loss of one race, all the rest have equal
   claim.

"Once to every man and nation comes the moment to decide,
In the strife of Truth with Falsehood, for the good or evil
   side;
Some great cause, God's *new* Messiah, offering each the
   bloom or blight,
Parts the goats upon the left hand, and the sheep upon the
   right,
And the choice goes by forever, 'twixt that darkness and
   that light."

It was on the 22d of September, 1863, that Schneider began his life in the camp, and in a letter, written September 24th, we have his first impressions: —

"Camp Casey, Va., Sept. 24th.

"What a new experience I have had, and how much I could tell you about these two days in camp! I am here on Arlington

Heights, in a beautiful position, commanding a view of Washington, Georgetown, and the river. I was kindly received here by the colonel and officers, all of whom are gentlemanly, and three or four college graduates.

"Our colonel is a graduate of Dartmouth, a fine man, only twenty-three years old."

When he became connected with the camp, the question of who should be chaplain was up for consideration, and almost immediately the thought arose somewhere (we do not know who originated it), why should not Schneider be chaplain?

At the time of his examination, promotion of some sort was promised, and there was a thought of making him adjutant.

Under date of September 28th, only six days after he was in camp, he thus writes: —

"I was called to the colonel's tent to talk over matters. He spoke of the adjutancy, and asked about my voice. He spoke about the chaplaincy, and my obtaining a license to preach. I would like the adjutancy, but I question whether it is not my duty to be chaplain. Another puzzling question. I have prayed that God would determine it for me. I am really puzzled about this matter. But I will think and pray."

About the same time he writes : — " Do you know what has led me to seek the chaplaincy ? I think I can do more good so. What an opportunity! Think of being the religious instructor of nine hundred men! Then to have the opportunity to speak to them, or rather teach them, on week days."

In due time the chaplaincy was given him, and he came back to Massachusetts, — to Bridgewater, where he was now best known, — and a Congregational council was called to consider the question of ordaining him to the work of the gospel ministry. It was a peculiar case, as he had never technically studied theology, though his mind was richly stored with theological truth. The council met at Bridgewater, October 27th, and, after a full examination, he was duly ordained and set apart for the work of the ministry, with the understanding that if he should return from the war, he would then pursue his theological studies in due form. It was an occasion of great and touching interest. Rev. Dr. Dutton, from New Haven, preached the sermon, and Rev. B. G. Northrop made the ordaining prayer. This done, he returned to his regiment, and entered upon his work.

A little while afterwards, Col. Fellows, in writing home to his parents, then living in Lancaster, Mass. says: — " Your minister may know my chaplain. He was formerly a second lieutenant in my regiment but, on his being ordained, I gave him the chaplaincy (the highest rank I can really appoint, that is, cavalry captain). He is the son of Dr. Schneider, the celebrated missionary in Turkey. Chaplain S. was born in Turkey, has travelled considerably in the East, came to this country, and completed his education at Yale College, was professor at Bridgewater Normal School for a time, and, on entering the army, was about to take a tutorship at Yale, and in connection pursue his studies for a missionary to the East. He is the best army chaplain I ever saw."

It will be remembered, in a passage quoted from Schneider's letters, a little while ago, that he spoke of " three or four " college graduates among the officers of the regiment. That letter was written soon after he came into camp, and before he knew much concerning the officers. Col. Fellows, in the letter from which we have made the above extract, says: — "I have seven or eight college graduates, and only four from civil life. The rest have all seen service, and several of them hard times. Several were at Gettysburg. I have a captain who was captain there. He saw the color-bearer shot down several times, when he seized the colors and carried them through the battle. One of my lieutenants has been in eighteen fights. Including myself, there are now thirty-six commissioned officers in the regiment, and about nine hundred and fifty men."

On Sunday, Nov. 15th, young Schneider held his first regular preaching service with the regiment. He describes the day as follows: —

"I thought this morning, that we should have a rainy, and therefore a quiet in-door day of it. But soon the clouds scattered, and the sun came out brightly. I went up to the Hospital, taking two of the lieutenants to help sing, and held services. I think it did the men good. Very soon after dinner, I attended another burial-service, using the opportunity to speak a few words of warning. Soon after returning, dress-parade call was given, the square was formed, and I held my first regular service. We, a few of the officers, sung two stanzas of 'My country, 'tis of thee.' I read the ninety-first Psalm, and then spoke to them as soldiers, showing them how they stood before the world, what their present position and their future prospects were. They listened. After a short prayer, the whole battalion uncovering the head, I dismissed them with the benediction. After dismissal, one of the men came up to me saying, — 'Chaplain, dems was good words. It makes the boys all feel nice.' This evening, we had a very pleasant meeting here in my tent. The prayers were earnest and thoughtful."

About a week from this last-mentioned date the regiment received marching orders, and then came the bustle and confusion of breaking up the camp, and taking their departure.

CHAPTER VIII.

THE REGIMENT ORDERED SOUTH. GOES TO SHIP ISLAND.

THE order to move came at last somewhat suddenly. The regiment was to go to New York, and thence by steamer to New Orleans. A hasty letter, written by Col. Fellows to his parents, in pencil, on board the steamer "Continental," just as she was about to sail from New York, will give an idea of the whole movement up to that time. He says:— "I have had innumerable troubles, or delays, since I left Washington. The train was to be ready at daylight, Tuesday morning." [This was Tuesday, Nov. 24th.] " So I commenced to get ready at 12½ o'clock at night, and I was at the depot at 7½ A. M. We did not succeed in moving till 12 M. At Baltimore we had to change cars, besides marching a mile. At Havre de Grace we waited full two hours. At Philadelphia we had to march

THE REGIMENT ORDERED SOUTH. 139

another mile, from depot to depot, besides changing men and baggage to ferry-boat and to cars again. At Jersey city we waited a long time for the ferry to New York, and at last arrived in Park Barracks, on Broadway, at 10 P. M., Wednesday night."

The next day was Thanksgiving; and, during the early part of the day, it seemed probable that the regiment would not be ordered forward until the morrow. But the letter proceeds: — " When I was all settled for the night, came notice that I must move the regiment to the boat. So away we went, — marched up Broadway to Canal street, thence to Canal street wharf. A dense crowd followed us. The regiment was the 'lion,' all the while, in the city. No disturbance occurred, however. Two or three insulters were punished. One of the men knocked down a man for insulting an officer (calling him 'white nigger'). The adjutant knocked another down for insulting him. Once on our way by railroad (coming on to New York), our car was stoned. Such is our life. But we are all proud of our regiment. I am the first to lead a black regiment through the city of New

York. The movement was eminently successful."

The letters of Chaplain Schneider give full details of the voyage; but as there was nothing very peculiar in them we omit them. They reached New Orleans Dec. 4th, having had a quicker voyage than they anticipated, though with abundance of sea-sickness. In the letter written immediately after their arrival he says: — "All the way up the river we were most enthusiastically cheered by the inhabitants, especially the blacks. Oh the profound bows the black women made! — So ludicrous! . . . . We are going to Ship Island, to stay about a month."

Ship Island, whither they are going, is one of several islands in Mississippi Sound.

The regiment arrived there Dec. 10th, and, soon after reaching the place, he sends the following letter to his father: —

"MY DEAR FATHER, — This is the very last place I expected to find myself in. I remember that when Butler's expedition was stated to be stopping at Ship Island, I thought I would just look on the map; but I never imagined that I should see the island with my own eyes. It is about eleven miles long, and on an average a mile wide. It is about twenty miles from Mobile, and sixty from New Orleans by the Lake Pontchartrain route, and a hundred and eighty miles by the river route. The north-eastern part of the island I judge to be the oldest, from the fact that there is more vegetation on that part than on any other. All our wood comes from there, and indeed that is quite a troublesome matter, inasmuch as we have to transport our wood seven or eight miles, and as yet we have no teams to do it with. We need a little fire at night and in the morning. Our great want is wood to cook with. The men have actually only half enough to eat, because food could not be cooked. We are encamped at the south-western end, in company with another colored regiment, and under the guns of a fort which the government is building here. This is also a naval station, and several men-of-war are off here all the while. . . . .

"There is very little to distract the attention of the men, and they can study here to advantage. I have a large marquée, which will accommodate about seventy, and in this I hear my classes, and hold my prayer-meetings. I am at the same time studying for my own improvement. The Bible makes my particular study. I hope thereby to abbreviate my theological course, and to be in Turkey about as soon as I originally intended. Eddie is getting along nicely. He is economical. I think he is a *good boy*, too. He has improved. There is a good deal that is noble in his character. Father, I am glad you take such a view of my going to the war. It is a comfort.

"This is a short letter, but I will write again. God is very good to us. His greatest blessing to me is A.

"Your affectionate son,
"JAMES."

In order that we may the more fully illustrate the nature of the young chaplain's work, and the current of his thoughts and feelings, and thus justify, in some measure, the strong expression of Colonel Fellows, — " He is the best army chaplain I ever saw," — we propose now to give, somewhat continuously, his own account of his labors there, as gleaned from

his letters. December 10th, he writes: —
"I am sitting in the colonel's room at headquarters. We are not settled down yet, and so, for a while, we of the staff make this our rendezvous. There are quite a number of houses in the island occupied by the other regiment. Our colonel, however, has the principal house, surrounded by a veranda, and crowned by a cupola. He has only one room, and here we are, the colonel, major, quartermaster, adjutant, and I. We have good times here, agreeing vrey well. Last night we had a very pleasant, intelligent talk together, all smoking except the quarter-master and myself. But, to entertain us all, the colonel had oranges produced and discussed. I like the colonel more and more. He spoke to the officers on the steamer last Sunday, and said he wanted them, all of them, to attend services in the cabin. I may not have told you that I then gave an informal lecture on a variety of subjects, vulgarity of conversation, etc. They listened well, and afterward fell to discussing the topics themselves. Yesterday morning, we buried two more men who died in consequence of exposure during the voyage. I said a few words

at the grave. Military forms of burial tend to give importance to *death*, and so value to life. This is most essential. War depreciates life."

Dec. 11th he writes: —" Yesterday I pitched my tent. And a most magnificent tent it is. It is a Sibley tent, with two very large tents on each side. At any time, by drawing down the partitions, it may be divided into three tents. One end I use as my private tent. The other two I shall use for my school-room, and chapel. This is a God-send to me. It is just what I want. The colonel gave it to me. He will do almost everything for me that I wish. This place and these circumstances are very propitious to my work, and if we stay here for some time, and I have health, and God blesses me, much good, I hope, will be done. My mind is full of plans and purposes. I am studying, and thinking, and working, with hand and tongue."

The next letter is dated Dec. 16th: —" I have taken several walks upon the beach, and have found considerable Natural History awaiting my consideration. I have found three species of jelly-fish, and have also examined a horse-shoe crab. I have at length organized my classes, and they are in working order. I have two classes of beginners, and one of more advanced scholars. I give them eight hours a week. All my evenings are taken up. On Sunday and Thursday evenings, prayer-meetings with officers; on Tuesday evening, one with the men; on Saturday, lyceum; and on the other evenings, classes. The lyceum, too, is in operation. I drew up the constitution, and organized the whole thing through. Almost all the officers will be in it. We discuss the confiscation act next Saturday. I find some time, say two hours a day, to read."

Dec. 17th he writes: — "We had a prayer-meeting as usual this evening. Very earnest prayers were offered, and petitions and thanks too for 'our chaplain.' One plan after another suggests itself to me. I'm going to lecture to the men, once or twice a week, upon common topics. The men are glad to do anything for me. My post-office business takes up a good deal of my time. But I am glad to superintend the matter, because the men's letters are poorly directed, and unless some one sees to it, they will never reach their destination."

Dec. 22d he writes:—" We had a pleasant day last Sunday, and I preached to the regiment. I spoke on the subject of economy. These men are most wasteful, much more so than other soldiers. The colonel spoke afterwards on the same subject. In the evening we had one of the most interesting prayer-meetings we have ever held. There was a good number of officers present, and, as soon as the meeting was thrown open, one man immediately offered prayer, and then another, and another; then some earnest, heartfelt remarks were made, and then an officer, who has been leading a most errant life, offered a repentant prayer. The effect was most excellent. After meeting, a number of them sat down, and we had a very pleasant talk. You know that the officers take charge of the Sunday evening meeting. I ask different men to take charge, and I am trying to get those who do not frequently take part, to take charge, so as to 'work them in,' as they say. I am thinking now more especially of this subject: the various means to be devised to secure a constant spiritual growth, — a systematic, progressive, Christian life. I wish to write several sermons on the subject, to be used not only now, but also when I am studying theology. I must write one or two lectures on secular subjects."

From a letter written January 7th, 1864, we take the following: — "My desire to go out to Turkey increases. Paul's intense missionary spirit produces a kindred desire in me, and I find that I am thinking of the work, not as a duty, but as a happy privilege, and now my thoughts and studies all tend to that work. This present work and situation is doing me good in this particular. I do not know, however; there *may* be work for me here in America. I wait patiently.

"Please send me some papers. We have not had a northern paper since we have been on the island. We wish to see the President's message, — his proclamation. We have gathered scraps of it. How grand the war looks in its results! Do you not see them all? God! God! All our wonder, all our worship, all our thoughts, end in Him. Blessed be his name!"

January 8th he says: — "I rode down to the fort with the colonel this morning and as the morning was bright, the air strongly oxygenated, our horses in good spirits, and the beach hardened by the receding waters, we enjoyed it much. After dinner, I fixed up my 'fly,' and then visited the hospital, reading the Bible and newspapers to the men, talking and praying with them. Reading the President's message in the earlier part of the evening, I went down to the meetings of the men, in their company streets, and then, collecting my choir, practised some hymns."

The following is to his sister Eliza: —

"Ship Island, Jan. 9, 1864.

"My own, only Sister, — Precious Lizzie, — Just now I was thinking to whom I had written by this mail; and when I thought that I had written to A——, to Auntie, Willie, Edward, Charlie, and other business letters, and that my precious sister Lizzie alone was left out, the tears came running down my cheeks. No, my sister, not because I have ceased to love you is this. You are more precious than ever. This separation only endears my friends. A—— tells you all the news, I suppose. Is she well? Does she look happy and cheerful, or is she fading away? It is too bad; I ought not, perhaps, to have come away. . . . Tell A—— that we are going to move up to the upper end of the island, and that I am going to have a smaller and more convenient tent. That marquée has been an elephant on my hands. To keep it standing in the wind, and warm in the cold, has absorbed all my energies. Would you believe that the water freezes in our tents, every morning, now? The men have really suffered from the lack of wood. I think the other regiment will move away, and we shall occupy the fort and the barracks. One thing is very convenient, — by digging two feet into the sand and setting down a barrel, we have a well of sweet water. This white sand is an excellent filterer, as William will tell you. We are studying Natural History at a great rate. I must stop now, dear Lizzy, and get ready for our lyceum. I often think how much you and William (Rev. Mr. Dwight) have done and are doing for your family friends. Thank you and him, good man that he is. My love to him and Harry.

"Your brother,
"JAMES."

In a letter, written January 25th, he says: — "Saturday was a most beautiful day, — the clouds all below the horizon, the air still, the sun genially warm. I took a short walk, after breakfast, in the woods, and was sung into worship by the sweet birds. I asked the colonel at noon to give me more time at the service, and we arranged that dress-parade, on Sunday, should come an hour earlier than usual, thus giving an hour for service afterwards. I preached upon *stealing*, — a thing that is egregiously common in the regiment. I don't write out my sermons. I simply sit down and think them out, and then speak them off without even a skeleton. I do not fail to bring out most that I have thought of. The evening prayer-meeting was very solemn and impressive. There is progress and development in some of the Christian officers. The lyceum, too, has a good influence. It stimulates the mind; I can see it plainly.

They prayed very earnestly and cordially for their chaplain. After meeting, I went to take part in the meeting of the men. What do you think I saw? In one very large gathering, they were singing and shouting very earnestly, and almost dancing as they sung. I saw there was something of special interest going on, and stood outside. Soon, I saw in the midst a man lying on a litter, and apparently in great mental agony, crying out — 'God have mercy! God have mercy!' There were three men singing and chanting and praying around this man, *exorcising* him, *bringing him through*. What do you say to that? Ninety per cent. of this religious zeal is, I believe, nervous or magnetic excitement. I took no part, except to ask the Christians there to pray still more for that man, as the meeting broke up. I am learning much of the peculiarities of these men by going around among them every day. I meet with difficulties. The men are very much attached to these peculiarities of worship, which I know to be injurious. I must use management."

January 29th he writes of a tragedy among them: — " Last Friday, one of the coolest premeditated murders was committed, in our regiment, that I have ever known of. Two of our men had a quarrel in the afternoon; hard words passed between them, and a blow was struck. The insulter, who was struck, but was really the man to be blamed, swore revenge. At evening, when the company was falling in for dress-parade, the man took his place much nearer to the victim of his passion, and, turning around, coolly took aim and shot the sergeant as he stood in his place behind and at the right of his company. The ball went through the man's chest, and he fell and expired in a few seconds. We buried the unfortunate man yesterday. The funeral was, of course, largely attended, and I improved the opportunity to speak of the nature of the crime, and of the *anger* and abusive language which led to it. I asked myself, as I stood beside Sergeant Wang, last Friday, 'Am I responsible for this man's soul, if it is lost? Could I have done something to save him?' And the answer was, 'When you preached upon *stealing*, you might have preached Christ and the way of salvation.' And so, yesterday, I thought I could delay no longer, and preached,

'Believe in the Lord Jesus Christ.' I gathered statistics last week, and found out that not much more than a hundred out of nine hundred of the men are Christians, while a little more than half the officers are Christians. Do you not think there was reason for my preaching so? I think the effect was good. In the evening, the prayer-meeting of the officers was very interesting. I think there is at least some spiritual interest at present. Before the meeting, I attended a meeting of the men."

In his letter, February 3d, we find the following pleasant and beautiful thoughts: — "I am in one of my most pleasurable states of mental excitement, which are caused by the inflowing of new and good thoughts, and which so thoroughly wake me up that I cannot sleep for a long time. I have been meditating upon the life of Christ. I believe that *woman's* character, whenever brought into contact with his, is resplendent with amiable virtues. Women never doubt or question; women stand by him when the fidelity of men proves false; women never insult him arrogantly and with pride. They are speechless, humble, and still so powerful in faith that they secure divine interposition in favor of others. Call to mind the woman at Jacob's well; the woman taken in adultery; the woman who anointed his feet in Simon's house; Mary of Bethany; Mary, his own mother. How sweetly humble the answer of the Syrophenician woman, — 'Yea, Lord, yet the dogs under the table eat of the children's crumbs.' I think I am gaining much by this study; I love Christ more. Jesus, I think, is a sweeter name than Christ. Jesus means Saviour."

February 11th he says: — "This Thursday noon I called together the Christians of the regiment, to talk with them about matters of religious interest in the regiment. I was surprised to see so large a response to my invitation. I asked men of the different companies to tell me how matters stood with them, and so we arrived at the fact, that there were between twenty and twenty-five 'mourners,' or inquirers, in the regiment. I then gave them some suggestions as to the manner of conducting their meetings. I frankly told them that I was not accustomed to their method of conducting meetings, and had not been so educated; but that they must not infer that I thought their way wrong or inexpedient. I assured them that I had the deepest interest in their growth and enlargement. I told them that whenever I could, I should come down to their meetings, and conduct them through the first part, and then leave the meeting in their hands. This, I think, is the best plan. I will read the Bible and explain it, and *start* them with new thoughts, and then they can carry themselves to such a pitch of excitement as they choose. This afternoon I went down to the lower end, and made arrangements to preach to the prisoners on the island, many of whom are from white regiments in this department, sent here under sentence of court martial. They number about sixty."

The extracts which we have thus made are largely from letters to a single individual; but his letters to Aintab, to his friends at Englewood, to his mother, who is still in this country, during the earlier part of his stay on the island, all breathe the same spirit, and abound with the same essential details. He is exceedingly busy and laborious in his work. To his mother he writes, just before her departure : — "I love the missionary work. I read Paul, and he makes me a better missionary. I really long for the work now, as I did not awhile ago. God sparing me, I will go right on with my studies as soon as my war-work is done. Dear father! bless him for being willing that both his sons should go into the fight."

In a letter to his father he says : —

"MY DEAR FATHER, — We are still, you see, on this quiet island. We have moved our camp from the western end to the woods which cover the eastern half of the island; and whereas we suffered from the want of wood at the other place, we now have a plenty of it, and besides have a little verdure to soften the glaring of the sand. We are all very comfortable now, and have had bright, sunny weather these four weeks. The men are in good health, — are dressing neater, and keep their arms in good condition. Very providentially we have had good weather for four successive Sundays, and I have preached every time.

"I may not have told you that the regiment is drawn up in the form of a square, whenever the weather will permit, and I speak to men and officers all together. I thus have an audience of seven hundred, more or less. My position is somewhat difficult. The men, in their ignorance, need very simple preaching, while the officers, who are above the average in education and intelligence, need the highest style of preaching. But as the men are more numerous, and by far the most needy, I address myself to them; but at the same time try to make my simple language convey valuable and not common truths.

"My subjects are simple and elementary, — my texts, hitherto, the ten commandments. Do you not think this kind of work may fit me for missionary life? I am still teaching, you must remember, and am learning how to teach all the while. This, too, fits me for the peculiar work in Turkey, which I have in mind. My heart is upon that work, father, much more than it used to be. My present work leads me into it. How do I know but that, if I had kept on with my studies, I might have become so ambitious a scholar, I might have been unwilling to go out as a missionary?" . . . .

Frequent letters also went from him to his brother William, who was connected with the navy, and held the office of assistant engineer on board the steamer "Calypso." But we must not extend these extracts.

He had written, about the middle of February, that they were immediately to leave Ship Island; but his last dispatch from that place is dated February 16th, and is as follows: —

"You see that we are still on this island, notwithstanding the postscript that I wrote on the outside of my last letter. As I told you, I went down with the letters, and finding that the boat did not go back till noon, I sat down and wrote another letter. In the mean time, dispatches brought by the boat had gone up to the colonel, and, as I wrote, he came down with the news that he was ordered to Key West. We all like the change. To be sure, the climate may not be as good. But we shall be near a city,—shall have regular communication with New York, and shall be within six days of you. We are now probably permanently fixed. We give up all idea of going into the field."

So ends his story at Ship Island.

CHAPTER IX.

REGIMENT REMOVED TO KEY WEST.

THE stay at Ship Island had been prolonged beyond the time originally anticipated. It was a little more than two months that the regiment remained there. It had been an excellent place for the chaplain's work, and the opportunity had been thoroughly improved. February 17th seems to have been the day of breaking up there, and on February 22d the regiment enters the harbor at Key West, — an island off the southern point of Florida. A letter from Chaplain Schneider, written that day, will give his first impressions of the place: —

"Rising this morning we soon saw Key West light; then Key West itself was in sight, and soon a pilot came on board, and we steamed into the harbor. The waters of the harbor are sea-green on account of the coral bottom. It is on the western end of the island, which is about seven miles long, and runs east and west. Fort Taylor, which we are to garrison, is situated on the south-western end, at the entrance of the harbor. (I am now writing in the cabin, as we lay anchored in the harbor, the colonel having gone ashore to receive orders.) This is Washington's birth-day, you know, and all the vessels in the harbor are gayly decorated with flags. There are a large number of all manner of craft lying here; several gunboats, — the San Jacinto, and the famous slaver, Wanderer, among the number. Tugs and row-boats are plying in all directions. Of the houses we see little, as they are mostly hidden by the banana and cocoa trees. The fort, of which we as yet know little, looks formidable, has three tiers of casemated guns, and is said to have two hundred guns. The day is most beautiful. The air is most genial, and we are happy. We are glad to be once more in civilized life. It is pleasant to hear once more the whistle of the railroad engine. There is a railroad running from the fort to two market towns near the eastern end of the island. Key West will open a new life to me, and I must address myself to it with earnestness. . . . .

"I hope that God will spare me to come back, and go on with my studies. I pray for that.

"Our general commanding this district of 'Key West and Tortugas' is Woodbury, a very fine man, — a Christian."

February 26th he writes again: — "Only *four* of our ten companies are in the fort. Another is in barracks, and the other five are in camp, awaiting the completion of barracks which will accommodate all. The camp is about a mile and a quarter from the fort. I can of necessity be with one battalion only. I am a little sorry for this, but I will try to distribute my labors. *All* the companies, however, will attend in the fort *on Sunday*. The fort-yard will be an easy place for me to speak in.

"Almost the first thing that the general asked the colonel, when he reported to him for duty, was whether he had a good chaplain, and an important question with him seemed to be, where our men would go to church. He at once invited the colonel and myself to dine with him. We found him a very agreeable, intelligent, scholarly man, and an earnest Christian. I had to refuse wine, although the general urged it upon me as the purest of wines; and after all he did manage to make me take some, by pouring it himself on the sugar on my plate, saying it would make good sauce. We had a very pleasant talk. They have three interesting children. His wife is a very elegant lady.

"The arrival of a colored regiment in a southern city creates a little uncomfortable feeling among the inhabitants, and at first we may encounter opposition and contumely. But we are really *masters* of the city, and will put down all opposition."

We have also several of the letters which Colonel Fellows wrote to his parents, during his life at Key West, and a few brief extracts from these may help us to know the character of the place, as respects natural position and scenery, as also the character of the inhabitants.

He says: — " We landed and encamped under orders from Brigadier General Woodbury, commanding ' District of Key West and Tor-

tugas.' Found the people very bitter against
' niggers;' but did not care much. The 47th
Pennsylvania volunteers, whom I relieved,
were also very much opposed to us. They
used every sort of epithet against me, as did
also the citizens. Yet some of the people
have called upon me, and when I grasped their
hands, I felt that friends were around. . . .
Key West is the most beautiful spot I ever
saw. Everything is green, and the warm air
and pleasant breezes are delightful. I only
wish you could see me as I am now located."

When it was known that a colored regiment
was coming, a petition was circulated and
signed by white soldiers and by citizens, asking the United States government to interpose
and remove the regiment from the place because they were negroes. Colonel Fellows
says, in view of this: — "If I should attempt
to interfere, I might commit offence, so I only
await further orders, confident that *I* never
defrauded the government while in its service,
and that *I* am loyal. These things, and such
as these, make me an abolitionist. I first declared myself one, when a *man* in a United
States uniform was brought into the central

guard-house (at Washington), bruised and injured, because, as the secret police said, he was a 'nigger.' .... Since I have been in my present position, I have been insulted, cursed, and abused everywhere. But to-day I am proud that I am here. I only wish I could command this district myself. No man would curse the government openly in the streets. .... I am ready for the field, and would ask no better men to lead. But my men are happy and comfortable, and here I can solve the great problem, better than anywhere else, as to their capacity for becoming soldiers. .... Here I can teach them manhood, self-reliance, — not only how to be soldiers but how to be gentlemen."

On the 2d of March, eight days after the arrival at Key West, Chaplain Schneider writes : — " I have organized my classes again, and this time on an entirely different principle. Out of each company I select three or more teachers, — *competent* teachers, and allow each of them to teach six of their company, giving them fifty cents a month for each scholar. I superintend the work, and have the teachers recite to me. The money for paying these teachers will be taken from the post fund, which mainly comes from savings on flour rations."

On the 4th of March he writes: — "I have been around, seeing the prisoners. There are some thirty of them, confined for various offences, political and criminal. There are men here confined from suspicion, — there are rebel soldiers, murderers, thieves, mutineers. Prisoners are liable to be very much neglected. They are confined very long before trial, and then they are passed from one hand to another, without thought or care. They become filthy, and often their spirit is broken, and they don't care what becomes of them. I shall try to see them often, and talk with them, and give them reading whenever they can read. I frequently visit the hospital, too. It is a general hospital, and men from almost any regiment may be left here by transports which pass by the place. One of our own sergeants is very sick, and knows that he cannot live, and he feels that he is not ready to go. I saw him day before yesterday, and he sent for me yesterday. He is in great anguish of mind, and cannot bring himself to

believe that Christ is willing to forgive him.
I prayed with him, and led him toward Christ,
as well as I knew how. We buried a man
yesterday, and bury another to-day."

Then follow the experiences for March 4th
and 5th.

"This is Saturday, and I am busy in writing out in principal heads what I shall say to-morrow. I shall preach upon lying; and to the colored people of the city, upon Paul's exemplary life of labor for Christ. Whenever I undertake to write a sermon, I am forced to go to God." . . . . "I have been quite busy, having preached for the colored people this morning, and for the regiment this afternoon. I was so busy all last week, that I had not made much preparation for the Sabbath till yesterday morning. I was glad that I preached to the colored people. The house was well filled (it is a small church), and they listened well, and seemed affected for good. Soldiers were there, and sailors, too. I shall preach for them regularly,—once every Sabbath. I shall find a large field of labor here, and I shall do all I can."

In a letter of March 10th he says: — "We have just returned from our prayer-meeting, at the other camp. I have written a little of my sermon to-day, and this afternoon have visited the hospital and prison. I seem to have very much to do, but after it is all done, it seems to amount to little. Well, the only remedy is to work harder. I want to preach a good strong sermon the next time. I want to organize the colored churches, too, — to unite the Baptist and Methodist in one society."

Again he writes: — "This is the thirteenth of March, and to-morrow I shall be twenty-five years old! A quarter of a century old! Shall I see another quarter of a century? If I do, it will probably be the best part of my life. How much ought a man to do in so much time? But shall I ever see it? But why need we trouble ourselves about this uncertain future? We will take the present and work now."

We might also give many extracts from his letters, showing the interest he took, and the progress he made in the study of the natural objects about him, trees, plants, shells, etc.

In March, he, with a friend, sailed to the Tortugas, for the purpose of gathering natural curiosities, and, especially, specimens of coral, which there abound and are very fine. He says: —" My plan is, to study zoölogy and botany, so far as to have a good understanding of the outlines of these sciences, and so be able to study them by observation all through life. Chemistry can only be studied in the laboratory, but all the other sciences need only a watchful eye. I am becoming more and more interested all the while." His description of this journey, and of what he found, is too long to be here inserted, but he felt on returning that he had greatly widened his range of knowledge."

Again he writes: — " This is my day for visiting hospitals, and this I did to-day, attending a funeral at the same time. I have many funerals to attend, and as I read some new passage each time, and try to think of some new ideas appropriate to the occasion, I find that I am exhausting my thoughts, if not the passages. To-day I have formed a sort of system of progressive sermonizing. All subjects for sermons may be brought under three classes : God and his character, — man and human nature, — and the relations between God and man. A minister should form a conception of God's attributes, and preach upon each in succession, and should have two or more series on these subjects."

A few brief extracts from the letters of Col. Fellows, written in March, and among the early days of April, will show how things looked from his point of view : — " The people of Key West flock in crowds to see my men, and they are getting more liberal ; for they say, they must confess, they can drill better than the veteran Forty-seventh Pennsylvania, which were here before. They (the men) behave well too. I have a great quantity of work to be done in the way of cleaning, etc., before I shall be perfectly free to let things take their course." . . . " I am mounting guns, and doing all I can to put the armament of the fort on the best footing. A great deal of polishing must be done, and things must be kept clean, both as a matter of discipline and health." . . . " My men have excellent quarters. That is a great satisfaction. I never am contented as long as I feel they are at all uncomfortable. I have walked about among them many a time, to make them feel better, by letting them know that I appreciated their troubles. Here, I have nothing of that kind to do. The fort is as sweet a place as I ever saw. But I am using lime plentifully." . . . " I hope we shall have no fever here. Every precaution has been taken against it. I am now putting the fort in a good sanitary condition, and shall pay particular attention to the barracks of the men." . . . "The days are getting quite warm here. Sometimes it is fearfully hot. Yet a west breeze is always blowing. Tropical fruits are plenty, — oranges, lemons, bananas, cocoa-nuts, etc."

All the letters that come from Key West about this time, though they are, on the whole, hopeful, are tinged with a certain apprehension about fever. The following interesting letter was written by Chaplain Schneider about this time to his father: —

"FORT TAYLOR, KEY WEST (FLA.), March 15, 1864.

"MY DEAR FATHER, — You will be surprised to see my letter dated at this place. I am sure we no more expected to be sent here than we expected to be sent to Ship Island. We sailed into this harbor on the 22d of February, and in three days were marched into the fort. You know that this island and the Dry Tortugas are considered the key of the Gulf, and, in the event of a foreign war, would be invaluable. Indeed, when we were threatened with war with Great Britain, the forces on the island were tripled. The rebels thought they were sure of having the place; but they were too dilatory in trying to possess themselves of it. And, even if they had taken the place, they could not have kept it long, because our fleet could have cut off all supplies from the island, and could have thus starved them out. But as long as we have a navy to bring supplies, we can hold the place against almost any force. Notwithstanding we have always had possession of the place, the citizens are almost all of them in sympathy with the rebels. They lost their slaves by the President's emancipation proclamation, and are particularly bitter against all blacks, and most of all against black soldiers. As soon as they heard that a colored regiment was coming to relieve the regiment already garrisoning the place, they sent a petition to Washington, asking that the order be countermanded. They hate us thoroughly. They insult us too, and in such a way that we cannot have them punished.

"The colored people of the place are in sad want of teaching and preaching. They have been driven from the churches, in which they were members. They now worship by themselves. I preach for them every Sunday, and will do for them all I can. We hope to change the public opinion of the place by gradual means. It may be surprising that such incipient treason should be tolerated in a city, totally dependent upon the government for support. But this is the case in many places, and many officials are still in partial sympathy with the secessionists.

"I find much to do among my own men. They take a new interest in the matter of learning to read and write. We have very good places for study here in the fort. Our rooms, too, are very capacious and comfortable. We live in elegant style. I am studying zoölogy and botany; for you know the fauna and flora of this latitude are very different from those of ours. I am studying heavy artillery, too. I am more than ever interested in the study of the Bible. I want to accomplish very much. The yellow fever, you must know, often appears here; but it was almost entirely prevented by strict quarantine regulations last summer, and may be averted by cleanliness and careful diet; and we can go north in the sickliest part of the year. I have just entered upon the twenty-sixth year of my life. Can you believe that you have children twenty, and twenty-eight, and (it might have been) thirty years old. May God help me to live a holier life, these coming twelve months.

. . . . I hear from William occasionally. He is working hard. I presume you and dear auntie are, by this time, on your way to Aintab again. I wish A. and I were already settled down there. I want to be about my life-work; but God has given me something to do for the present. He will guide us. Pray for us, dear father. Auntie has very much endeared herself to us. Very precious is she to us all. God keep you both, dear father, and gather our whole family to himself at last. " Very affectionately,

" J. H. Schneider."

We have, also, a letter to his brother William: —

"Fort Taylor, Key West, March 29, 1864.

"My dear Brother Willie, — I have recently received two letters from you, both dated at Norfolk. I think it much more likely that we shall meet each other here than at Ship Island. Navy vessels are coming in and going out almost every day, and there were very many of the vessels in the harbor, and very many of the officers on shore, about the hotels, when we arrived. I begin to understand navy life a little. I see that many lazy, worthless fellows find their way into easy, lucrative positions in the navy. A naval officer seems to be more a gentleman of leisure than military officers. They are more delicate in build, — more gentlemen, in *external appearance*, I mean.

"We like the place very much. The yellow fever can be kept out, they say, by strict quarantine regulations. Well, whether the terrible epidemic comes or not, we have been sent here, and we shall stay cheerfully, even in the midst of numerous deaths. The fort is a magnificent one, and our quarters very agreeable. But I have told you all this in another letter.

Nothing remarkable transpires here. Now and then, miserable bands of refugees come over from the main land, and take the oath, and find work upon the public buildings. The smaller a place is, the more gossip there is afloat; and so it is here. Every man's hand is against his brother, socially, and scandal is unlimited.

"Eddie is finally in the army. He has not written me since I gave him permission to enlist, and so I do not know whether he got the bounty. He is in Co. K., 57th Massachusetts. We must write to him frequently, and keep him in good counsel. He will see hard times. I hope he will have health.

"I think I shall go home on a furlough in July. Can you find your way up to New York about the same time? I am glad that you feel the need of Christian sympathy. It shows that you are living a Christian life. We all learn lessons in mixing with men. I wonder sometimes that *grown* men betray weakness; but it is mainly because they have not been thrown into circumstances which try the trait of character in question. A *strong* man,— let me see him, — I mean, strong in moral and mental force. I heartily commend your honest ambitions, your studious habits. All of us boys are now in the war, and I guess we have the average of patriotism in the family. Write soon.

"Very affectionately,
"JAMES H. SCHNEIDER."

The three brief extracts which follow are from letters written March 31st, April 1st and 2d: — "This morning I wrote on my sermon, and in the afternoon read a little in Gray, and wrote my quarterly report, and before tea attempted to make two calls, but succeeded only in the one upon the general's wife, Mrs. Woodbury. This evening we have had our prayer-meeting. Thus far, this week, I have been able to do things in the proper time."
. . . "I have to think out very simple things for our men, you know; but my plan is to write out a more elaborate sermon each time that I speak to them, and then use this when I preach to more intelligent audiences." . . .
"We have had north winds, of late, and the weather is very comfortable and healthy. We anticipate a safe summer. There is very

much in keeping one's mind calm and fearless.
We feel that our lives are in God's hands,
and that we are safe. Most assuredly, we are
in God's keeping; but it is sometimes hard to
trust."

On the 8th of April he wrote, and the following is a brief extract from his letter: —
"I have had a talk with the general about the
schools of the place, and he asked me to interest myself in the matter, and do all I could.
He does not seem to think that there is any
need of a *free school*. I intend to look around,
and plead hard for a free school, if there is
really need of one. Last night we went up to
a prayer-meeting, at the other battalion; but
they had not got through receiving pay, so we
gave the prayer-meeting up, and, on my way
back passed by the colored church, where there
was a prayer-meeting, and Captain Lincoln
and I went in and took part. Another day is
gone, and its history is recorded. In heaven,
I imagine, we shall take much less note of
time. I am certain we shall not mourn over
past time or lost time."

April 10th he writes: — "This has been a
happy Sabbath. I went up to the church and

it was filled very well. Many of the women brought their children. I had spoken to them about it, and encouraged them to accustom their children to visit the house of God. The size of my audience cannot be much enlarged, because the house is filled, galleries and all. They listened very well, and seemed to understand and feel. I preached upon this: — 'Take my yoke upon you, for my yoke is easy.' After service the people were very cordial, and seemed to think that I was their friend.

"This afternoon we buried one of Captain Lincoln's men, and after I had spoken to them, I asked the captain to say something. I like to hear him. He is a good Christian man. From the graveyard, I went over to the other battalion, and held service there. I have lately got up a reading-room for the men. I gather the papers of the officers, after they have read them, and file them, and lay them on a table in one of the ordnance rooms. This will incite the men to study more."

Again, on the 12th of April, he writes: — "As to the yellow fever, we do not expect it here this summer. The weather, thus far, has been very favorable. The city is being thoroughly policed, and the quarantine regulations are rigid. But, after all, if it does come, we will commit ourselves to God. He will do well, and justly, and lovingly. We are trying to live unto him. I feel more and more like Paul wishing to give up everything for Christ."

We are listening now to the last words that will come to us from this dear and loving brother; and let us note particularly his beautiful spirit, and his earnest zeal for the Great Master, even to the very last.

The three following passages are from letters bearing date, respectively, April 13th, 14th, and 17th.

"I have just finished the study of the Epistle to the Galatians. I am trying to form an idea of the object and purport of every epistle, and finally of every book in the Bible. I think I am loving the work of a minister more and more. I am looking forward to the missionary work with increasing pleasure. I want to give up all for Christ, to suffer with him, so as to conform to him. I want to emulate and imitate Paul, the prisoner of Christ.

My scholarship, my love of study, all this is too little to give to Christ. I wish I had *more*. I will try to have more, so as to give it to Christ. It is blessed. We should be willing to inherit the promised blessings and benedictions. There is a great dearth, or lack of the martyr spirit; not that which comes from false religious pride, but from love of Christ. So, finding a large field of usefulness in this place, I am willing to labor, even at the risk of life, for Christ's sake." .... " I have thought a little, to-day, of my talk to the men on Sunday. I have studied, too, both Ephesians and Philippians. This morning I wrote to Miss M. about her Christian experience, urging her to give herself at once to Christ. I wanted to do something at once for Christ. This afternoon I have been around among the colored people, urging them to attend the church, — comforting the sick, explaining the means of salvation, arguing with a colored Catholic, commending the general industry and frugality of the blacks, conferring with committee-men about building a church and school-house for the blacks. Have I told you that I have organized a writing class, for the non-commissioned officers, which I meet every day, after dinner, in company B.'s mess-room? I am trying to do a great deal, but accomplish little."

. . . . " Saturday, in order to encourage the colored people to contribute toward the building of their church, I promised to secure one dollar for them for every five that they should raise. I can get this in the regiment and elsewhere. The church is to be used as a school-house, too. I think we must make these people help themselves, but encourage them all we can by assisting them. The people are very depraved and vicious on this island. Drinking-saloons are numerous. Sabbath-breaking is almost the general practice. I think I shall be thoroughly initiated in the practical part of a minister's work."

On the 19th of April he wrote a letter, from which we take the following brief passage: — "I have just returned from my writing-class. They are doing well, and seem to be interested. There are some very bright scholars among them; one of them, Richard B., is particularly so. Captain Lincoln has taken a class among the men, and hears them daily.

He is one of the most active Christians I have ever met. I am perfectly well and happy."

And here this story of Christian love and Christian labor suddenly stops. It must be left to others to give the sad and painful sequel.

CHAPTER X.

SUDDEN DEATH. — LETTERS OF CONDOLENCE.

THE narrative of his life, as drawn from himself, stops, as we have said, April 19th; but these earnest labors in behalf of others went on two days longer, until Thursday, April 21st, when he was suddenly stricken down with fever, and died on the following Tuesday, April 26th. Notwithstanding all the hope which had been expressed, the yellow fever was there early in the season, and the loving, laborious chaplain was among the first to fall. The same day on which he died, Capt. Lincoln breaks the sad intelligence in a letter to A—— : —

"KEY WEST (FLA.), April 26, 1864.

. . . . . "At the request of our chaplain, Mr. Schneider, I am about to write you. Last Thursday he was attending to his duties as usual, but towards evening complained of feeling unwell. He had severe pains in his back and limbs, and also in his head. Nearly all the night he was delirious, and had little rest. We called in our surgeon, who prescribed for him, but he did not seem to improve. Friday he was in much less pain but very weak. He continued so until Saturday; then, by the doctor's orders, he was removed to the Post Hospital. I visited him there Sunday, and found he did not gain, although Sunday night he slept well and for a long time. Monday I again called to see him, and felt there was little chance of his recovery; therefore, at his request, I sat down to write you, but retained the letter, because I wished to send you more favorable news. The mail not leaving, I kept it until this morning, and now I have to convey to you the sad intelligence that, last night, Mr. Schneider was called home to the good Father. We prayed for him, and asked God, if it were possible, to restore him to health again; but the Father hath taken him to himself.

"Monday, I visited him, in order to take any message he might have to send to his loved ones at home; but his mind wandered, and I could not talk to him without exciting him greatly. You may be assured that he had loving friends here, who have done all they could to comfort and assist him, and who miss him as a brother. His loss is very great to us. We know it never can be replaced. None can work as he did, or take such an interest in those about him.

"I pray that you in this great sorrow may find comfort and consolation in the Word of God.

"Your friend,
"BENJ. C. LINCOLN,
"Capt. 2d U. S. C. T.

"P. S. He died from that great scourge the yellow fever."

The same day Lieutenant Reinhardt wrote to Rev. Mr. Dwight, as follows: —

"KEY WEST (FLA.), April 26, 1864.

"REV. MR. DWIGHT: DEAR SIR, — In your present great affliction, occasioned by the death of your relative, the Rev. Mr. Schneider, it may be a comfort to his friends at home to know how universally beloved and respected he was in this regiment.

"This is my motive in addressing a few lines to you, though I have not the pleasure of being personally acquainted with you.

"Our chaplain's death has spread a sadness over the whole regiment. His earnest and devoted Christianity, his warm heart and gentle spirit, and his courteous manner have gained him the affections and esteem of both officers and men.

"My quarters being near his, I have enjoyed his society perhaps as much as any of us, and many pleasant hours have I spent in conversation with him.

"The day before he was taken sick he was urged by some officers to act as counsel, at a general court martial, for a man accused of murder. He consented, and I, who was a member of the court, noticed that the case affected and excited him somewhat. In the afternoon of the same day he attended the funeral of one of our men, and at the grave he addressed his hearers with his usual warmth and earnestness. It was his last public service, and I shall always remember the solemn words, in which he pointed out the Saviour, to whom his soul was so soon to take its flight.

"I will not attempt to offer consolation. There is One, with whom both Mrs. Dwight and you are well acquainted, who can comfort you infinitely better. May He be your comfort now and forever. Assuring Mrs. Dwight and you of my deep sympathy and esteem, I am, dear sir,

"Very respectfully,
"Your obedient servant,
"J. C. REINHARDT,
"Lt. 2d Regt. U. S. Col. Troops."

The man who wrote this truly neat, courteous Christian epistle, as might be inferred from his name, was a German, and, only a few weeks after, was called to bow to the grave before this same fell destroyer.

The mail, which brought the above letters, brought also the public letter to the "New York Herald," from its correspondent, Mr. Slack, stationed at that time at Key West. His death was therefore announced in the "Herald," May 5th, about the same time that the private letters reached Englewood. The writer for the "Herald," speaking of his death, and glancing briefly at his early history, says:— "I heard Mr.

Schneider preach to a few companies of his swarthy congregation, on the green sward, before the United States barracks, one evening, and I must certainly say that, without descending to any low language, he adapted his words wonderfully to his audience. His sermon contained no points of abstract doctrine, nothing political, nothing to tickle. It was sound good common sense. In fact, it was a practical sermon, full of good advice to the men he addressed. He will be buried, I believe, to-morrow morning without any pomp or parade. Peace be to his ashes!"

Two days later, Major Townsend, who afterwards became colonel of the regiment, writes as follows: —

"U. S. BARRACKS, KEY WEST (FLA.), April 28, 1864.

"REV. MR. DWIGHT: DEAR SIR, — It devolves upon me, as the major of the regiment, to inform you of the sad fate of the late Chaplain James H. Schneider. Regrets are vain, but we wish to bear testimony to the respect and love we bore him. He was the light of the regiment, and it had scarce been lighted, ere the Lord has seen fit to extinguish it. We can never supply his place. There is not one minister of the gospel in a thousand who would do the good that he has done in the regiment. There are exceeding few who are as well calculated to fill the same place, with the same degree of credit.

"We mourn his loss and tender our sympathies to his bereaved relatives and friends at home. In writing thus, I feel that I do but give expression to the sentiment of the entire regiment, officers and men. . . . .

"Mr. Schneider died on the morning of the 26th inst., at three o'clock. The physicians differ in opinion as to the nature of the disease, some pronouncing it the yellow fever; others are of a contrary opinion. The symptoms were in many respects those of the yellow fever. . .

"I remain, with great respect and sympathy,
"Your most obedient servant,
"BENJ. R. TOWNSEND,
"Major 2d Regt. U. S. C. T."

The doubts, which were at first expressed as to the nature of the disease, soon gave way before the fearful tide of events that followed.

It was natural for men, situated as they were, to try and think this was not yellow fever.

Col. Fellows, writing May 10th to his parents, says, in words ominously brief: — " Chaplain Schneider died, very suddenly, two weeks ago to-day. There is a diversity of opinion as to whether he had the fever or not." In this way Col. Fellows was trying, if possible, to quiet the fears of parents and of another, very dear to him, all of whom he knew would be full of trembling anxiety, now that they had heard of young Schneider's death.

It devolved upon Rev. James H. Dwight, the elder brother, to transmit this sad news to Aintab. He writes as follows: —

"Englewood, May 5, 1864.

" Dear Father, — The hand of God has again fallen heavily upon our family circle, and with deep sorrow I have to communicate the message which has just reached us from the army. Your son James has been removed from earthly scenes, for God has taken him to himself.

" It has come upon us with a fearful suddenness, as it will to you. That one so noble and faithful in his zeal for God and for his country, should be so early cut down in his youth, and the promise of great future usefulness in the earthly field of Christ's kingdom, where the faithful are so few, — be crushed by death, — is one of those mysteries before which we stand in awe, and can only meet, in our deep sadness, by humble submission to the will of the great Father.

"It is not for me to urge the consolations of Christ, to one of your experience in communion with the Blessed Master, in hours of trial. But I may tell you that James was faithful to the end, endearing himself to all around him, and dies lamented greatly by the officers and men of his regiment.

"He had obtained among them a noble name for his earnestness in the ministry of the gospel." [We omit details already stated in letters from Key West.]

"His last letters have been very cheerful, and he urged repeatedly that there was no danger from yellow fever, as it had not appeared. He must have been one of the first victims. Our information is through a Capt. Lincoln, who was one of his best friends, is a good Christian brother, and was with him much of the time.

"As you may imagine, the blow has fallen with fearful weight upon our dear sister A—. . Her heart was bound up in him, and she has been laboring for some time under a presentiment that he would never return. Eliza is sustained by her care and anxiety for A—.

"I have known but few young men of his age who seemed to combine so many great and good qualities as James. He was above all things deeply pious and filled with the noblest purposes. Added to this was a strong intellect, cultivated and rich; for he has always improved his privileges. We have had reason to expect that he would make a powerful and eloquent preacher. He was amiable in all his dealings with those around him, and endeared himself to every one that knew him. What more can I say?

"He is now with the other loved ones who have gone before, and soon we shall meet him and them in that blessed land where no more death can enter. I must now close. You will receive other letters soon, and we will give you whatever particulars may reach us.

"All the rest are well, and send much love to

all. William and Eddie were well at the last dates.

"Your affectionate son,
"JAMES H. DWIGHT."

But we must go back for a moment to Key West; for this death was but the beginning of sorrows there. The disease went on its way, rapidly striking down one and another of the officers of the regiment. On the 15th of May, Col. Fellows writes his last letter home, and in it, though he tried hard to be cheerful and of good courage, it was plain to be seen that he felt the awfully depressing influence of the place. His regiment had been in a measure scattered, — some parts of it having been sent in one direction and another, inland, on various expeditions. He says: — "I am not very desirous of seeing bloody fields, or of active service. I do not long for it; and yet I must confess that I should like to be put in some position where I would have more duties to attend to, and not be left to the wilting of this hot sun of Key West. I would like to see my regiment together again, as it was on Ship Island, and not scattered over one hundred miles of Florida." Hardly had this letter been despatched to the north, when he, too, fell suddenly before this terrific disease, — the only son and eldest child of his father's house, — greatly beloved in his own home, and dear as life itself to another, whose fortunes and hopes were bound up in him.

A second letter from Capt. Lincoln, written June 15th, will more fully explain the circumstances of Mr. Schneider's death, and will at the same time give us a glimpse of what had since been passing there.

"KEY WEST (FLA.), June 15, 1864.

. . "You may think that I have taken too long to answer your letter of the 17th of May. But you will be satisfied it was not from lack of inclination, when I inform you that I have been sick with the fever which has proved so fatal to so many of our officers.

"Since our late chaplain died, we have lost our colonel, Capt. Reinhardt (but lately promoted), and three lieutenants, besides our sutler, and one lieutenant is still very sick. Every officer that has been in the fort for any length of time, with one exception, has been sick with the disease, and no others: so it would seem that something in the fort occasioned the epidemic. I presume more than five hundred men were sick, but only four of the men died. It seldom proves fatal to colored men.

"You ask me if Mr. Schneider was exposed to the disease. I think that being in the fort is sufficient reason for his sickness. I believe, however, that, a short time before his death, he was present when two of our surgeons examined the body of a soldier who had died very suddenly, and it is probable that this was a case of yellow fever; and his being present at the *post mortem* may have caused the sickness of Mr. S., although he would have had it subsequently, I think, because, as I before mentioned, every officer, except one, quartered in the fort, has had the disease. You ask if Mr. S. apprehended death. The very first evening of his sickness, in his delirium, he talked about the yellow fever, and afterward, although the surgeons did not for some time consider it a case of this kind, Mr. S persisted in believing it to be yellow fever, which was the case. He suffered very much at times, during his illness, and his case was the most violent of any our surgeons have attended.

"I think it was the second day of his sickness he requested me to write you, giving me your address. He said, 'Write her as cheerful as you can.' I do not think he thought, at that time, that he would die; if he had, he would have sent some last words to you. After his illness became more alarming, I dared not speak to him of you, because I knew it would make him much worse. In this disease the mind has a remarkable influence upon the body, and when the patient gets the idea into his head that he will not recover, no medicine can save him. As he (Mr. S.) was very nervous, I did not care to increase it by talking to him. The day before he died 1 did go to the hospital for the purpose of receiving any message he might wish to send to you and his friends; but his mind wandered, and 1 could not talk to him. . . . . And now I have written all I can recollect in regard to the last days of our loved friend. I would I could see you a short time, and then I could perhaps answer many questions it is not easy for you to ask in a letter. If I come north this fall, as I hope to do, I will, if possible, call upon you, and if ever I can be of service to you, in any way, I shall be most happy, for the esteem and regard which I had for our chaplain. I always speak of him as 'our chaplain,' because I admired him for his faithfulness in that position, and have seen the good work which he has performed in our regiment. . .

"Please remember me to Mr. and Mrs. Dwight.

"Your sincere friend,
"BENJ. C. LINCOLN."

The following tender and sympathetic letter came from a college classmate: —

"HUDSON, N. Y., May 23, 1864.

"MY DEAR MR. DWIGHT, — Yours of the 7th instant, containing the mournfully terrible, sad intelligence and particulars of James's death, came to me duly. But my pen has not moved easily to a reply.

"There were so many years of our intimate acquaintance; so much life-history which we had made together; so much that neither could ever forget; so much that has now become tender memory; so much thought of him now; so much that it would be a mournful pleasure to say to those who are so crushingly bereaved,— that I do not know how to say anything, and have it only the little that can be put in a letter. . . . .

"I ought not to speak of my own sense of loss to those who have lost a brother, and to her who has lost — *all*. May God help her, is our earnest prayer. We both send to her, and to yourself and wife, and to James's brothers, our deep sympathy; and our hearts go across the sea where this blow will fall so heavily.

"I have never lost a friend so intimate before. We were *chums* during most of my Andover days, and even more intimate at Yale. I knew him thoroughly. He confided everything to me, — much that he never trusted to any other, as he used often to say. How many hours we spent together! I never knew either of my brothers half so fully as I knew James. . . . .

"How hard it is to realize that he will not come again! I used to know his step, on the flag-walk near my room, from any other; but, I fear I am writing childishly. I cannot well write manfully of him now. And you all have so much greater burden to bear, you will hardly think I have any place among those who mourn for him; but he was so near to me, he seems a large part of my history.

"How much you all have to comfort you in view of his rare Christian character, you know well. I can truly say, I know no classmate so ready to die as James. It is saying much, but not at all too much. When he was in Hudson, last year, I was more than ever impressed with the earnestness and thoroughness of his Christian life. I always considered his whole character one of remarkable simplicity and sincerity; and what is rarer in this world than simplicity of character? But I need not write thus to you, who knew him so well. May He, who only can, help you all to bear this heavy load of sorrow.

"Say to A—— (we always call her so), that we shall not forget her in our prayers. What else can we say to her? Mrs. McKay will write to her. . . . .

"Yours, sincerely.
"E. DeCost McKay."

This mournful news reached Aintab June 11th, and Dr. Schneider writes in reply, forgetting, in a measure, his own grief, in his effort to comfort others: —

"Aintab, June 14, 1864.

"My darling Daughter Eliza,— Since the startling news of dear James's death reached us, June 11th, I have thought much of you. I know you will feel the bereavement as keenly as any of us. The death of dear Susie was a very heavy stroke to you. Then came the death of your darling babe. And now, so unexpectedly and suddenly, has your much-loved brother been called home. All these sorrows have come to you with great bitterness and poignancy. Your tender and sympathetic nature, I know, must feel all this very deeply. But while you must and will feel desolate, remember, my dear child, that, as even so small an event as the falling of a sparrow occurs not without our heavenly Father's notice; so, an event like this, affecting so many of His own children, and especially in your case so directly, has not occurred without His direct interference. 'He is too wise to err, too good to be unkind.'

There are also very many attending circumstances which alleviate the bitterness of the cup. Your mind will easily call them up. My heart bleeds, almost, as I think of the thousands, all over our land, who have been called upon to mourn those who have fallen in the recent battles without giving any evidence of preparedness. We, on the other hand, have the most comforting hope of James. Dear child, lift up your eyes to the everlasting hills; exercise faith in God,— in his goodness and mercy. Believe that, in some way which we cannot now see, his death will be for the good of Christ's work and for God's glory. Do not constantly look on the dark side of the picture, but also on the bright one, for it has some comforting views. I wish I could be with you to speak some words of comfort to your heart. Well, I can pray for you, and this I do. Your dear Aunt Susie feels the stroke most deeply. She had become deeply attached to James, and mourns for him as for a first-born. I have great anxiety for Eddie. As far as I am informed, he is in Burnside's corps; and in the severe fight near Spotsylvania, Tuesday, May 10th, it is said, 'Burnside precipitated his whole command upon the rebels, and terribly cut them up.' I suppose Eddie must have been in this fight, and, if he escaped without a wound or death, we shall have great cause for gratitude. I am very anxious to get our next letters and papers, to learn the particulars. Our American dates go up as far as May 14th. As I have foreseen, the campaign will be the bloodiest of the whole series. May it make an end of slavery, and the blessings of peace soon follow! You, or some of you, must not fail to tell us all about Willie and Eddie. The extracts from their letters are exceedingly interesting to us. Love to all.

"Your sympathizing
"Father."

In closing this chapter, we must make a few extracts from one letter more, which tells its own sad and pitiful tale:—

"My precious Father and Mother,—May I call you by these dear names? My heart clings to you in its great sorrow,—turned to you at once, so soon as I could think of any one; for, in the suddenness of the first bitter grief, I seemed almost paralyzed, as if my life must go with his. . . . Just when life seemed so bright and beautiful, — when the cherished hopes of years seemed just about to be realized, in an instant they were all blighted. . . . The hardest thing has been that I could have no last word, — nothing after those letters written in perfect health. I have felt, if I could only have been with him in the hours of sickness and death, or even, if this had been denied me, if I might know just what his views and feelings were in those last hours, — could have received some parting message, — I could not ask more. But I must not ask this. God has afflicted me, and he has done it in his own way. We must see that it is his own work. . . . .

"The thought may come to you, as it did to me, was it right for him to enter the army? But I cannot doubt it. Even you, dear Aunt Susie, would not doubt, could you read his letters written at the time, and see how strong were his convictions that he should go. I have read over all his letters (my treasures), and I see that he first thought seriously of it a year ago last summer, after his return from Lake

George, while he was studying at Bridgewater, a week or two before the term commenced. One afternoon he devoted entirely to thinking of it, and he decided that it was not his present duty to go. Eddie seemed to be then the principal cause of his so deciding. But he felt that, in staying, he was solemnly called to live more earnestly and faithfully, and the last year at Bridgewater was a witness of the accomplishment of this. He was anxious, and labored for the conversion of his scholars as never before. Then, when the draft was anticipated last summer, for weeks before, he wrote of it, always saying he should go if he were drafted. And it was a subject of prayer with us both, and we felt that it would be God's call if indeed he were drafted. But he did not really think he should be; and the question was a very painful one when it came, especially as he had to decide contrary to the opinions of some of his dearest friends. He thought he would not go, at first; but was very unhappy in this,— felt that it was wrong. When, however, he finally decided to go, he did not waver for one moment, — was perfectly happy; and I think his last seven months were the happiest of his life. . . . .

"My heart aches for you, . . . for I know how you have for many years looked forward to his joining you in your work. How your hearts have rested in him! . . . . And then I have been rebuked in fearing that you would be overwhelmed with grief, — in doubting that God would grant his sustaining grace to you, his well-tried servants, when he has so mercifully given it to me. Oh, I never knew before, the preciousness of a Saviour's love! It has been everything to me. Without this, there was no comfort. It seems impossible to me that one could live through such a trial without the Saviour's love to sustain. . . .

"Eliza is very precious. She seems almost sacred to me now, as the nearest James. Much as I have always loved her, she is far dearer now. Perhaps it will be some comfort to you to know that all a sister can do for her it will be always my greatest joy to do, and I think it may be permitted me, in the years to come, to do much to lighten her toils. I love to do for her as for no one else. In those first sorrowful days she dried her own tears for my sake, — left everything and came home with me, and stayed over Sunday, and comforted me more than any one else could. God will bless her." . . . .

CHAPTER XI.

TESTIMONIALS OF CLASSMATES AND VARIOUS FRIENDS.

FOR two or three chapters back, the work of unfolding the character and life-history of young Schneider, has been taken mainly from the hands of the writer, and entrusted to others. We have known of no truer or better way of making known what he was than by allowing him to tell his own story, and permitting those freely to speak who were intimately associated with him. In this closing chapter we shall pursue the same method.

These testimonials will come from various directions, but they will all bear conclusively upon the same great point. Some of these might, with perfect propriety, have been introduced into the previous chapter, as being letters of condolence, written soon after his death. But in making our selection of passages from this class of communications, we shall aim, as a general rule, to omit that which is merely sympathetic, and take those parts which bear testimony as to his character. Others of these papers have been furnished by request that they might find a place in this volume.

We will first make some extracts from letters written at Bridgewater, or by persons who had known him at Bridgewater.

Mrs. I. W. Boyden, wife of the principal, writes, under date of May 12th, 1864:—
"We feel that a beloved brother has gone from us. Three years of mutual labor and interest greatly endeared Mr. Boyden and Mr. Schneider to each other, and I do not think that the tidings of the death of an own brother would have so overcome Mr. B. as this. . . . . His pupils here feel his death very severely; and the impression made upon his scholars, the church here, and many more, by his life, his teachings, and his earnest prayers, I feel, will never be obliterated. None who knew him here, but loved him more than an ordinary friend. In the church, on Sunday, when his death was announced, there

were few eyes but wept. Old men and women, who had never spoken with him, but who had heard him say, 'Our Father,' in the prayer-meeting, wept as if they had lost a close friend, and those who knew him intimately felt that a brother beloved had been taken from them. Miss Comstock and myself were speaking of him, and of his labors for and with his pupils, and she said : 'He was ripening for heaven, and why did not we know it? Our eyes were holden, that we should not see it until now.' But, oh, how glad we all are, and ever shall be, that we knew him so well,— that we had his influence and his example and his affectionate interest ! "

Miss L. Comstock, a teacher at Bridgewater, referred to in the foregoing communication, writes on the same day, May 12th : — " My woman's heart goes out to you with such a strong, resistless flow of sympathy, in this hour of your great sorrow, that I cannot forbear its expression. . . . . . The cloud, which rests so heavily upon you, spreads far and wide, for few were valued and loved as he was. Trembling words and tearful faces give daily proof of the hold he had upon the affections of those who came within the reach of his influence. That influence! — do you know what a power it was, stimulating, elevating, purifying those who looked to him as a teacher? I thank God he has given me one such friend, and has let me see how an earnest, noble, Christian man can live."

Miss E. B. Woodward, another teacher, writes, on the nation's anniversary day, July 4th: —
"My heart has yearned towards you in these long weeks in which you have been struggling with the bitter waters; but I have shrunk from offering you words of comfort, knowing there are griefs too bitter for human sympathy, when even the voices of dearest friends seem almost to mock the desolation; and when the greatness and the suddenness of the blow make the heart dumb before Him who dealt it, until it can open itself to the divine consolation. . . . . You probably heard from James of the manner in which he spent this anniversary in the two last years; and as I turn my thoughts to the gathering in the same place to-day, the scenes of last year come before me, and I hear again the eloquent, burning words, by which he pledged himself to his country, if

she should call for him. It seems a long year since then; and how full it has been! A lifetime almost was crowded into it for many. I think there was for James. I think his life, which seemed constantly to increase in earnestness from the time I first knew him, was intensified from that time. I interpreted it that his Christian zeal urged him to unusual faithfulness in prospect of a change of relations,— leaving us for Yale,— but a letter from Miss Kilbourn says, 'I wonder we did not know he was finishing his last work.'"

Miss E. P. Daman, a daughter in the family where he boarded, in Bridgewater, gives the following tender and touching tribute to his memory: — "When the news reached us of Mr. Schneider's death, our hearts gave a great throb of agony, and we looked in each other's faces, saying, with quivering voices, 'Not our Mr. Schneider,— it cannot be.' . . . Not until we knew that we should see his face here no more, did we realize how closely he was associated with our daily life. Our Sabbath evening songs, which we always sang after tea, are all reminders of him; and in many of them we can almost hear his voice, as we used to.

In my little flower-garden, at the table, and in nearly every room in the house, we find something that reminds us of some kind word or act; for his kindness was unfailing. It was not permitted him to leave any last words, but they were not needed. The testimony of his whole life is sufficient. No one could know him as we did, and see the beautiful simplicity of his daily life, — the earnest Christian spirit that showed itself at all times and in all circumstances, without feeling that he was ready for the summons to 'come up higher.'"

Miss Mary E. Robinson, one of his pupils, writes from East Dennis, Mass., Jan. 14th, 1865. She says: — "I was a member of the Normal School, at Bridgewater, during the last eighteen months of Mr. Schneider's connection with it. I was also a member of his Bible-class. As I look back upon those months I feel grateful to my heavenly Father that I was permitted to go there, and, most of all, that I was allowed to know Mr. S. so well, — to associate with him, — to be influenced by him. I had been there but a short time before I learned to admire him as a scholar; next, to honor and respect him as a teacher; and, finally, to love him as a kind and sympathizing Christian friend. Words alone can never express what I owe to him."

The following, which is in some sense an accidental tribute, will be read with much interest: —

"EAST BLOOMFIELD, N. Y., July 25, 1864.

"REV. B. SCHNEIDER, D. D.: DEAR SIR,— Allow me to introduce myself as an officer of the 2d U. S. Colored Troops,— as a friend and companion, and, at Key West, a room-mate of your son James. Dr. William Goodell preached here a few Sabbaths since, and, learning that I had sustained such relations to your son, advised me to write you. I do so with great pleasure, for I hold James's memory as sacred; and I rejoice to be able to bestow upon a missionary of Christ any consolation or joy.

"My acquaintance with James begins with his joining the regiment, as second lieutenant, last autumn, at Camp Casey, Va. He at once became known as an active Christian,— organizing a prayer-meeting, and, by personal effort, gathering the officers into it. It was his earnest piety that first suggested to us that he would make a good chaplain; and that position was accordingly very soon offered him. Besides the services of the Sabbath, James began a prayer-meeting for the men, and also schools for every evening (not given to the officers' or men's prayer-meetings), the object of which was teaching the colored men to read and write, etc. No Sabbath preaching, no prayer-meeting, no school was ever neglected or dropped. It was a sacrifice for him to forego his evenings, which might have been devoted to study; but he yielded them willingly. It was not pleasant (so others thought) to make one's tent a public place; but our chaplain fitted up rude seats in his tent, and welcomed every soldier that came for aid or instruction.

"During the winter at Ship Island, Miss., he continued the schools, etc., and was mainly instrumental in organizing a debating-club, which continued during our stay on the island. James was our best debater. He spoke pointedly, and had always given the subject a careful study. He always spoke as if he were in search of the truth, and not for the sake of controversy, or to gain the decision for his 'side.' And I may here remark that he was singularly candid and truthful in character. He did not assume to know or to be what he knew not, or what he *was* not. I have often talked with him upon his peculiar work among these colored men,— upon the best method of influencing them religiously and intellectually. He used to visit their private company prayer-meetings, which they carried on in their own way; but he at length decided that his presence was a damper upon their *over-fervid* exercises, and he left them to themselves, endeavoring, at the weekly prayer-meeting and upon the Sabbath, gradually to give them higher and truer notions of worship. Thus he was ever studying what to do and how to do it.

"At Key West, feeling that too few of the men could be under his own instruction, he formed the plan of hiring those that could read to teach those that could not, giving each teacher a class, and paying him three dollars per month, from the regimental fund. I was told that some three hundred of the men had learned to read since the organization of the regiment.

"James also started a reading-room for the men. Two or three weeks before his death I was ordered to New Orleans, and he sent by me for school-books, and also earnestly requested me to get some entertaining reading matter for the men.

"It was a great object with him to *educate* the men, — to develop their minds as a means of every kind of good to them.

"I was taken with the fever on board the boat, and after a long sickness was sent north, and never saw James again. I remember, just before my departure, that, at a prayer-meeting, James said in effect: — 'We are now living where life is very uncertain, and this should make us live for Jesus more earnestly than ever.'

"James preached to the colored people of Key West, at the Baptist church. It was an unpopular thing; but he never thought of popularity, — he must do Christ's work. I have heard that the men felt the chaplain's death deeply. They knew that he was their friend, —

and no officer had such a hold upon the affections of the regiment.

"I remember going with James, at various times, to gather shells, and in search of the animal wonders of the sea. He was very fond of such studies, and had collected quite an assortment of such curiosities. He had a little work of Professor Agassiz, upon Natural History, which he was studying; but he told me, one day, that he must give up this outside study, and devote himself entirely to his work. As his room-mate, I can say that I think he never neglected or put off secret prayer and the study of the Bible. In fact, he devoted much time to this study, and sent to New Orleans, by me, for Barnes's Notes on some of the Epistles.

"As I thus think over the course of your son, I am struck with his straightforward and persevering character, — his uniform consistency. I shall cherish his memory, and feel that I have been taught a lesson which, God grant, may do me lasting good.

"May God support you, sir, in your double affliction.

"Many Christians in this country are sympathizing with and praying for you. God will administer his own consolations.

"I learn that James, while delirious with the fever, spoke Turkish. I suppose, however, that you have learned more fully of his last sickness than I have.

"May God bless you and your labors, is the prayer of

"E. P. ADAMS."

S. H. Taylor, LL. D., Principal of Phillips Academy, Andover, furnishes the following brief but explicit statement: — "James Schneider was a member of Phillips Academy about two years, at which he completed, in 1856, his course of study, preparatory for college. When he entered the academy he was diffident and modest almost to a fault. On this account his real merits, as a scholar, were not, at first, fully appreciated, as he had not always sufficient confidence in himself to show, at his recitations, all that he knew of them. But his teachers and fellow-students soon learned that his quiet and modest style of reciting was not to be taken as evidence that he was not master of his subject. Others, by their fluency and full self-possession, might show, at times, to better advantage; but, when it came to the close questioning and the sharp analysis, he was rarely if ever found wanting. He was an independent scholar; he thought and investigated for himself. He was a diligent student; he made the best use of his time, not studying by spasms and then relaxing all effort, as is too often the case in the earlier course of study. When he left the academy to enter college, he ranked as the third scholar in a class of fifty-five.

" In his general character, as well as in his studies, he was a model scholar, — gentle, kind, respectful, attentive to every duty that belongs to a pupil. So punctual was he at all his exercises, so blameless and orderly, that I cannot remember an instance when there was anything in his general deportment and spirit that I could have wished otherwise.

" Such traits and excellences won for him the fullest confidence and the highest respect of all who knew him; and his subsequent success as a scholar in college, and the respect in which he was there held, and his readiness to devote his life to the service of his country, will not surprise any one who knew him as a school-boy here."

The following clear and emphatic testimony is from a classmate, E. DeCost McKay, whose letter, in the previous chapter, will be remembered. From his long-continued and most intimate relations, no one is better entitled to speak on this subject than he: —

"James Henry Schneider was my most intimate friend. I knew him as I shall never know another. I knew him at Andover, at Phillips Academy, — " Old Phillips," — while preparing for college. He was there before me, and when I entered, — for the first time in my life from home, at school, and far away, among entire strangers, — the first smile and the first kind act came from him and made us friends. We were soon chums. We boarded together at the old Excelsior Club; at opposite sides of the same table we prepared every lesson in the Andover course. And so at Yale: together in Alumni Hall we passed the dreaded examination for admission to that institution. We took our meals side by side at the same table, in the never to-be-forgotten Mackerel Club. We joined the same societies,—.the same boating club; taught in the same Sabbath school, — a colored mission school; and, as our circle of intimate friends was to a great extent the same, were thrown together in innumerable associations, which now come thronging back to mind and fill the heart. He used often, at Yale, to come late in the evening to my room for a talk. (We were not chums in college.) He was too busy to come often; but when something special was on his mind, or he was very wearied, he was sure to come, and, as I sat in my room, I could always hear his coming step, at some distance, sounding distinctly on the flagging. I knew that step as well as I knew the sound of the chapel bell. It is so vivid now! It seems impossible to believe that years have come and gone since then, and that he has gone with them. I knew everything he knew of his life, — and of himself *more* than he knew. I knew the minutest details of his early life in heathen lands; of his long passage, by sail, to America; of his first schooldays at Thetford Academy, Vermont; of his entire life at Andover and Yale; his character, his aims, hopes, fears; the influences that guided and made him; his religious life and progress; his after-college plans, till he heard the voice of God calling him, born in the East, to the grand army of the Republic of the West,— all, and so much more not easily narrated, I know.

"He was, emphatically, a child of prayer. The greatest power with him was his mother's prayers; and they were an ever-present influence. They gave the key-note of his own religious life. I presume he never for a day forgot them. He seldom spoke of them,—but always in a way that showed their power over his life and aspirations. Every day of his life, before coming to America to be educated, she used to take him with her to her closet to pray with and for him. He never forgot those scenes and those prayers. He used to speak of the last ones, and the last *one* before she gave him up to years of separation, during his education in this country. There are other missionary mothers who know something of such prayers. These did not go unanswered. He became thoroughly religious. Not that he ever dreamed that so much was justly to be said of him, for he was so distrustful of his own heart and progress in the Christian life, as at times to cause great depression. In fact, distrust of self — of his motives, abilities, acquirements, — was one of his leading traits. His standard was the true one, and, of course, he felt himself far short of what he ought to be. Yet he was heartily and earnestly a Christian, in the fullest sense of the word. He did everything from Christian principle. Every lesson was a work for God. His Christianity permeated every act. He was a *Christian student.* Though always fond of a mirthful occasion, his habitual mood was serious. He was in earnest in everything. As a student, he was one of the most industrious, earnest, and patiently laborious I ever knew.

"He never made a recitation that was not perfect. He was inexorable in his demands upon himself. The utmost exactness and thoroughness of preparation for every recitation and every task was the least he would accept from himself. And yet I suppose it can be said that he actually never went into the recitation-room without fear and trembling.

"He loved exactness, and was miserable

over half-knowledge. He strove for a high stand in his class, but had no petty rivalry in it. It was his duty to do his best. And I can testify that a desire to gratify his parents and sisters was a powerful motive, with other higher ones. He loved to go the bottom of everything, — to know the reason why.

"Such thoroughness told upon his scholarship. At Andover and at Yale he was admitted by his rivals to be the best Greek, and probably was the best Latin, scholar in his class. Had he been as fond of mathematics and of English composition as of the classics, he could not have failed of the valedictory. He lacked in college somewhat of the general culture that many students seek for in college. He spent almost no time in general reading. He longed for knowledge; but that was to come after college discipline. The Bible, Webster's Dictionary, and one or two standard books were the extent of his collection of books, until near the end of the course. He believed that a college course is designed to call out and perfect the machinery of the mind, — to give working power, — not to store the mind then and there.

Yet his desire for knowledge was a perfect hunger and thirst. As a speaker he would have excelled, with the practice he would have had. He was surpassed by few in naturalness and expressiveness of gesture, and received a prize in college for speaking. During the weekly gathering of the students for declamation, when at Andover, his name was called by mistake, — it was not his turn to speak till the next week, — but he answered the call, to my great surprise, as I knew he had hardly selected his 'piece' for the next week, and had not made the slightest preparation; but he went to the platform with an unusual confidence, and gave a most impassioned appeal in the Turkish language, taking, as he afterwards explained, words without connection or sense, if translated, but given with all the earnestness of expression and gesture imaginable. It brought down the house tremendously, contrary to all rules, and saved him the trouble of preparing an English piece. A tutor at Yale once remarked to me, that, the first time he ever heard Schneider's voice in recitation, at the commencement of the college course, he knew, from something indefinably oriental in his voice and manner, that he was from the eastern hemisphere. Not only in scholarship was high excellence his unswerving aim; but in whatever he undertook. He was president of his class, presiding at all the many business meetings of the class in senior year with surprising ability. He was a most enthusiastic gymnast and boatman, striving as always for the highest excellence.

"As a man, a friend, a companion, he was always kind, genial, frank, with none of the so-called small vices; had a modest bearing, that made him friends everywhere. He never had an enemy, and certainly had the high esteem of every one who knew him. His attachments were strong. To his mother, father, sisters, and brothers his whole heart went out, and he '*loved* with a love which was more than love.' His mother's death soon after he entered college had a great effect upon him; and, later, the sudden death of a most tenderly loved sister was almost too great for him to bear. I have known many brothers devotedly attached to sisters, but I never knew of an instance of so great an influence exerted by sisters as by his. Their letters were a constant and marked stimulus. In the death of one of them and in the death of his mother he experienced the deepest affliction, and knew, in its fulness, the baptism of suffering. It often seemed to me, while in college, that God was disciplining him for some great work. And now it seems clear that God, meaning to take him early, was fitting him to go. It looks plain now that he was wanted for work beyond the valley. Most certain is it, that when death, like lightning out of the brightest sky, struck him, he was fit to go. From that close of life we must turn. God will make it plain. But sum up that life. It will not startle the busy world. It was not of it. It had not touched it. But did he live in vain? Is it hard to find a *living* power in such a life? How many may not that life win to God and noble living? How gloriously he died! The great world hardly noticed it; but the day is coming when to that life, and to every life unselfishly imperilled and nobly given up for the life of the nation, that nation will do particular honor. There were not many such given for it, and it will find them out. Of the hundreds of thousands who went to the grand army of freedom, how few were led by unmixed motives! Desire of position, adventure, fame, the bauble of war, had not the very slightest place with him. He had seen this nation from distant and dark lands, and *America* was more to him than to many born on its soil. He had seen its flag honored in foreign seas, and it was to him the emblem of the latest civilization and the best. When he came from benighted lands, he came bounding with love for it. And when, in the nation's struggle, the lot fell on him, he felt a divine call, and, fully realizing what might come, he assumed it. There will be found few examples of heroism so bright among all the shining names of the war. It was a life of no remarkable outer conditions, — like all beginnings of life; but in the midst of the selfish ambitions the war called out, his simple devotion to country and freedom comes to us like a strain of clear music through the din of battle. There is enough in that life to fill with pride and high content even the hearts that were broken. Liberty will yet gather her jewels, too, and wear them in her crown forever. But more than all this, and above all, is the Christian life, giving a full lustre to heroism. It is a diamond in the diadem of Liberty, and it shall shine as the stars forever and ever.

"Put it, then, above his head, where he lies at rest, at last, in the quietness and beauty of Greenwood,* — He lived for God! He died for Liberty."

The following carefully prepared and extended paper is from Mr. Oliver A. Kingsbury, an intimate and beloved classmate, now minister, living at Joliet, Ill. : —

"On the wall of my study hangs the photograph of that band of brothers who had formed a family circle for so great a part of their college course, and who, on the morning when that picture was taken, were together, all of them, for the last time. Among that group of faces is one which must impress the beholder as being the face of a serious, earnest man. In my album is another picture, taken two or three years later, of this same face. You see in it the evidence of gravity, a more mature

---

* In the autumn of 1866 his remains were brought from Key West, as were also, at the same time, those of Colonel Fellows. Schneider sleeps in Greenwood, — Colonel Fellows in his native town, Sandown, N. H.

expression. But it is still the same face, serious, earnest; and such, as I remember him, was James Schneider.

"I began to know him during the latter part of freshman year. But it was not till later in the course that I knew him at all well. We boarded together for about two years, I think, and, in the daily intercourse of the club, character would not fail to come out.

"As I recall his character now, I think seriousness and earnestness were the predominating traits. They were evident in all that he undertook; evident even in his sports; evident in his studies; evident in his religious development.

"He was one of a party of us, that, during the summer of our junior year, used to spend many of our half-holidays in boating. I remember, almost as distinctly as if it had been yesterday, one afternoon so spent. We had rowed down to Savin Rock, and, when we came to return, found both wind and tide dead against us. The six miles up to the city were, of course, no hardship to us; but it required hard and steady pulling. I was in the bow, and Schneider was pulling next to me. I can even now almost see his broad shoulders swaying backwards and forwards, as we pulled. Not once did he pause during all the hour and more that it took us to reach the dock. But this was merely his way in everything. A piece of work to be done, — then there must be no cessation of effort till it was accomplished.

"Of his earnestness in his studies, I need bear no record. It was that which gave him, in spite of some early disadvantages, the third honor in a class more than ordinarily able. He studied till he understood the matter in hand, not content with a mere surface knowledge that would sound glibly. He must understand. And his patient assiduity has its reward.

"And his earnestness, too, was evident in his religious development. I remember how, sometimes in our prayer-meetings, particularly in the 'entry' meetings, where but a few gathered, he would make some inquiry, or express some views that looked deeper than some of us were in the habit of going. He wanted to enter into the hidden things, — to understand, if possible, all that could be understood of the matters of religious thought and feeling which we were discussing. He was not content with surface views in religion, any more than in science. He wanted to enter into the deep things of God. He was thoroughly in earnest.

"I only had one opportunity of renewing and perfecting my acquaintance with him after our graduation. One of the greenest spots in memory will be of the day or two spent in his society, at the home of his sister, during the summer of 1861. He had then been teaching for a year at the Massachusetts Normal School, and the result of the year had been to broaden and develop him greatly; so much so, that, it was noticeable by all his more intimate friends among his classmates. But he was still the same earnest man. I remember that, as we sat talking in the summer twilight, he turned our thoughts away from the more passing gossip of the hour, into some channel of historical discussion. He wanted to be learning, when others would have been content with the enjoyment of the passing moment.

"I saw him but once after those two golden days; and then only upon the street for a moment. He went to his teaching again; and was winning, one by one, the honors he merited. But the call of his country — *his*, even though a foreign, heathen land had been his birthplace — the call of his country in her need, he could not pass unheeded. And here, too, his earnestness of character shone forth. He did not go to win renown, or to gratify ambition. He did not go because he loved martial glory, or because of any mercenary motive. He went because it seemed to him to be duty, — stern, hard duty though it was. He went, sundering many dear and strong ties. He went, declining much easier and safer paths which he could have trodden without blame, without any stain of unmanliness upon his character. He could not disobey the voice of duty, as he understood his call. So he entered the army of the republic as a private. His earnestness led him to any post that offered where he could serve his country.

"The next I heard of him he was the chaplain to one of our colored regiments. The next, — he was dead.

"As I think over those of our number whom the war carried into untimely graves, I can think of none who was more likely than he to have been a blessing to the world. He would have gone through life as sturdily as he pulled at his oar on that summer afternoon in the golden prime of our college days. He would have dug his way *through* difficulties, instead of skimming over them, just as he used to dig through his lessons. He would have been serious and earnest in all his plans and pursuits, just as when he made the season of friendly intercourse the opportunity of increasing his stock of knowledge. He would have sought to investigate, though reverently and submissively, the deep things of our holy faith, just as he used to seek to penetrate them in our little prayer-gatherings.

"But his work was done, even though to human eyes it seemed but scarcely begun; and 'he was not, for God took him.' It seems as if the best and bravest and truest of our class were going first. The 'stars' are gathering thickly along our list in the catalogue; and, as we turn to some of those starred names, we know that our friends are shining in the heaven above us, 'like the stars forever and ever.' To the life of none of those dear departed ones does my memory turn so readily for an example of patient, steady, conscientious earnestness, as to that of

"JAMES HENRY SCHNEIDER."

And, what shall we more say? After all this diversified testimony, drawn from so many different quarters, there is little need that we should pursue the subject farther. We might attempt some analysis of his character; but that is unnecessary. We are willing to leave it in that beautiful *concrete*, which the previous pages have so fully exhibited. We might seek to give a kind of summing-up of what he accomplished in his short life. But it would add nothing to the impression already upon the mind of the reader. Of one point we feel sure. Here was a young man of rare excellences of character. Here was a Christian young man, who, in his short day of active life, was truly a "burning and shining light," and he has left behind a light that will continue to shine all along his pathway.

If any young person reads this book, who has never yielded the heart to Christ, let us ask, if a Christian life does not look noble in the light of such an example? Have you no secret yearnings to turn from a life of worldly pleasure and indulgence, and emulate such an example? Is it not high and godlike thus to live for others, rather than for one's self? "He who will save his life shall lose it; but he that will lose his life for my sake shall find it."

And for that far-off missionary home in Aintab what shall we say? Though there is sadness in that dwelling, we know there is also a holy joy. A little light was kindled there, which has burned very brightly and beautifully, and will burn on into the years to come. Besides all the direct influence which has gone forth from that home to enlighten the dark Armenian mind around, an indirect influence has also been cast abroad upon the world, whose power and extent can never be measured. And we know that that missionary father, from the strong love he bears to Christ and mankind, from his sense of what was done for the world when slavery was overthrown, can look out from his Eastern home, across the great deep, to this, the land of his fathers, and with a full heart, can say, in the noble words of an English poet: * —

"An end at last! The echoes of the war —
The weary war beyond the western waves —
Die in the distance. Freedom's rising star
Beacons above a hundred thousand graves; —

* John Nichols.

"The graves of heroes who have won the fight,
　　Who, in the storming of the stubborn town,
　Have rung the marriage-peal of might and right,
　　And scaled the cliffs and cast the dragon down.

"Pæans of armies thrill across the sea,
　　Till Europe answers: — 'Let the struggle cease, —
　The bloody page is turned; the next may be
　　For ways of pleasantness and paths of peace!'

"A golden morn, — a dawn of better things, —
　　The olive-branch, — clasping of hands again, —
　A noble lesson read to conquering kings, —
　　A sky that tempests had not scoured in vain."

[In the early part of this volume it was stated, as will be remembered, that Rev. Thomas P. Johnston and wife left this country in company with Mr. and Mrs. Schneider, with the expectation of being fellow-laborers at Broosa. It was, however, ordered otherwise. But, in the course of the volume, mention has several times been made of Rev. Mr. Johnston. These two families, who went to the missionary field together, have had some singular coincidences in their subsequent experiences. The son of Mr. Johnston, William C. Johnston, was born the same year with James H. Schneider, and came to this country for his education about the same time. They entered Yale College together, in 1856, and graduated together in 1860. Young Johnston then went to Danville, Ky., to study theology ; was licensed to preach in the spring of 1862 ; became chaplain of the 13th regiment of Kentucky volunteers; was a very useful and popular chaplain, and strongly won the hearts of the men of his regiment; but, after a service of two or three months, died at Mumfordville, of typhoid pneumonia. Two daughters of Rev. Mr. Johnston were also educated at Miss Dutton's school, in New Haven.]

EDWARD M. SCHNEIDER.

CHAPTER I.

EARLY YEARS.

IN making this brief record of a brief and heroic life, we shall pass rapidly over those events which have been brought to view in the previous narrative. We shall not dwell, at any considerable length, upon the outward circumstances and conditions of his early years, since those who have read the foregoing biography of his elder brother will have all these things sufficiently in mind.

And yet, lest some, through their especial associations with the younger brother, should wish to peruse the story of his life before reading the other, it will be suitable that we should take a cursory survey of the scenes and events of his childhood and youth.

Edward M. Schneider, son of Benjamin and Eliza (Abbott) Schneider, was born on the 17th of August, 1846, in the ancient city of

Broosa, Asia Minor. He was the youngest in a family of five children; and at the age of two years and six months, his father was called, in the prosecution of his missionary work, to remove from Broosa to Aintab, a city in Northern Syria. When this removal took place the two daughters were placed at school in Constantinople, under the care and oversight of missionaries resident in that city; but the three boys went with their parents to Aintab. Between three and four years after this removal it was thought best that the four elder children should go home to America with their mother, — three of them to remain for their education, while the youngest of the four, William, would return with his mother, at the expiration of her visit. Edward, then less than six years old, accompanied the family from Aintab to Smyrna, the port of embarkation. Here they were met by his two sisters, who had been brought from Constantinople, and whom he now saw as if for the first time; for, young as he was when the family was broken up at Broosa, he would not be likely to retain anything more than a vague recollection of scenes and events then transpiring. Only a brief interview could here be allowed him; long enough, however, to make him feel the charm and delight of this sisterly companionship. He was a child, moreover, of a strongly emotional nature, of fervid imagination, and he found a peculiar pleasure in this brief reunion of the broken household. But the time was short. The hour of separation must soon come. With sad and longing eyes, he saw his mother, his brothers, and sisters go on board the vessel, and pass away out of his sight, on their voyage to a far-off land, while he went back alone, with his father, to the solitary house in Aintab.

To almost any child, of such an age, this would have been a bitter and sore trial. But to him, with his intensely affectionate nature, it was almost too much to be borne. If the reader can recall, from his early experiences, the restless and gnawing sensation of thorough home-sickness, and then remember that this was a case having many additional aggravations, he may conceive, in some measure, what this young heart then experienced. In the third chapter of the first part of this volume will be found an extract from the letter of his father, graphically describing the scene and the sorrows of his childish heart, occasioned by this family sundering.

For a year and a half he lived at Aintab alone with his father, — a father devotedly attached to his children, but pressed, at that time, beyond measure, with his public duties, so that it was only in the brief pauses of business that he could give himself to the instruction and amusement of the lonely boy. But long-continued grief is not natural to childhood. The glowing life within crowds off care and trouble, and makes for itself pleasures, even in the most unfavorable outward conditions. A child, too, of such an active imagination as his, lives in a realm of his own creation. He makes himself companions of whatever comes to hand. He sets forward, and superintends large enterprises in his little imitative world. There is nothing more pleasing than to watch the operations of a little child of lively and glowing fancy, moving about in this small sphere of his own creation, peopling it with persons, and animating it with great interests and enterprises, utterly absorbed with what is going forward, so that there is no sense of the lapse of time, or of the passing of outward events.

In the fall of 1853, when he was now seven years of age, his mother returned from America, bringing to him his old playmate and brother, William. Long abstinence had prepared him to enjoy, with the keenest relish, this renewal of companionship. Thus time passed on, for three years and a half, until, in the spring of 1856, his father, in his turn, started on a journey to his native land, taking William with him, this time to be left in America for the purposes of education. Edward was now again left alone with his mother, as he had before been with his father. But she, from her living a more in-door life, and from the fact that she had always taken upon herself more especially the care and education of the children, was much more of a companion to him than his father had been, or, from the nature of his duties, could be. From his mother, too, Edward had taken his strongly imaginative and enthusiastic nature. She could see the movements and impulses of her own young heart repeated in him.

There was much in such a kind of life as this

to feed and stimulate the imagination. It was not the life of an only child in a family. The condition of such an one is peculiar, and there is almost always something unique in the character thus formed. But the circumstances of this case were quite different. There were brothers and sisters, only they were not present. His fancy played round them in the far distance. His thoughts busied themselves with what they were saying and doing in that unknown world of America, — the land of his fathers, of which he had, all his life long, heard so much.

Thus matters went on for three or four months, when suddenly a dark and terrible cloud gathered about that lonely missionary house in Aintab. The mother, his only companion, sickened and died, and the boy was alone. Surely here was a child, to whom, through all his early years, had been allotted a strange course of experience. He was but ten years of age, and now he was in that great Asiatic world, with no blood relative within four thousand miles of him.

Dr. Pratt, who, at the time of Mrs. Schneider's death, was laboring in Aintab, under a heavy burden of care and responsibility, in Dr. Schneider's absence, gives the following account of the manner of her death, as also the manner of her previous life : —

"There was no long illness and gradual failing to prepare us for this. She had not *seemed* to be unusually feeble, though we knew that she (as all of us) was overtasking her powers. But disease came upon her suddenly, and in less than five days its work was done. The great impression upon the brain — at first intense headache, and then stupor passing into coma — prevented any conversation with her during her last illness. But we did not need this for our comfort. Her love for Christ and for souls, her burning zeal and unwearied perseverance, are known to all. I cannot give you a history of Mrs. Schneider's missionary life, but I hope some one else will do it. Very few missionary ladies, I believe, have been able to accomplish as much as only the five or six years of her life in Aintab have accomplished. She had an earnest desire for the salvation of every one she met, and was faithful in efforts for their eternal interests to a degree rarely witnessed. She did not fail to follow effort with supplication, for she was a woman of much prayer; and many a woman whom she met but once, at least for that once heard the living gospel of Christ. Old and young shared her affections, and heard her counsels and instructions with pleasure. Oh that the mantle of her zeal and faithfulness might fall on us, — that we might have her spirit of prayer and her earnest faith! We shall miss all this greatly at our station. She had gathered a school of about thirty girls, many of whom wept sorely at the funeral of their beloved teacher. I have no doubt that many souls, at the last, will rise up and call her blessed. She has done a great work in this place, and great will be her reward. Who will now do the work from which she is taken? Who will care for all these? The two ladies had as much as both could do, and now it has all come upon one. Oh that we had more strength and more helpers! We ask the churches to be helpers together with us in their prayers; especially that we may live more holy and unblamably before God, and serve the Master better and better from day to day."

The condition of the boy, left thus alone,

seemed sad enough ; but there were many near at hand who could be deeply touched with all the strange incidents of the case, and who were ready to afford such sympathy and relief as were in their power. So soon as the necessary arrangements could be made, it was thought best that Edward should go to Constantinople, and remain in the family of Dr. Dwight, until his father's return. But in that slow-moving Eastern world, with the great distance of Aintab from Constantinople, it required some time to perfect and carry out this arrangement.

His father did not return until the fall of 1858, — two years and a half from the time he left Aintab. Meanwhile he had been united in marriage to the sister of his former wife, and, on reaching Constantinople, Edward was introduced to his new mother, possessing qualities of character and heart not unlike those of his own dearly beloved mother.

He went back with them to the home in Aintab, — a home darkened for him by strange, sad memories, but now made cheerful again by the light of kind looks and winning voices. Still, he was the only child in the house. His new mother took her place in the household, and devoted herself especially to the business of his education and training. This she could do more exclusively even than her sister, especially during those early years, while she was yet obtaining a mastery over the language of the country; for, until this was effected, there was a barrier standing in the way of those various public labors for which the first Mrs. S. was so remarkable, and for which the present Mrs. S. is almost equally so, now that the impediment has been removed.

In 1861 began our dreadful civil war. As was said in the opening of this volume, the missionaries, from every part of the world, looked on with the most intense interest. Never were newspapers from America in such demand, in these scattered households over all the earth, as now. The great distances to be travelled made the newspapers old when they reached these dwellings; but they were fresh and new to them. By the necessities of the case, they must always be several weeks behind actual events, and this fact gave play to the imagination, as to what might have been happening between the time when the newspaper was issued and the time when it was read at these remote points of the world. Moreover, throughout all that Eastern world, so much nearer to England than to America, the intervals between the arrival of the American mails were filled with the doleful comments and prophesyings of the English press, notoriously unfair and hostile to the loyal cause; but, in the absence of more reliable information, this influence was fitted to cast a cloud of despondency over the minds of these faithful children of America, who, nevertheless, prayed on and hoped on, in spite of all delays and discouragements.

In this far-off missionary home at Aintab you might have heard just as minute details of all that had been passing in this country, — names of leading generals and other officers in both armies, — names of statesmen and prominent actors in every department of this public activity — as though you were conversing in one of the loyal homes of America. And so it was in other missionary dwellings in various parts of the world.

But it may be doubted whether, in any other remote household, anywhere in the world, you could have found a lad of fourteen years, upon whose thought and imagination the war took such a mighty hold as upon this solitary boy at Aintab. It absorbed every thought and emotion of his soul. When the time drew near for the arrival of another mail from America, his feeling of expectation was so intense, his curiosity to learn what had transpired was so absorbing, that he was almost beside himself with longing excitement. And when the papers came, they were not left until every shred of news was read, and not only read, but re-read and thoroughly mastered, so that not many American youth here at home could explain every feature of the situation as he could. And yet to him this was a foreign land. He had never set foot upon its shores. He knew of its geography and shape only by studying the maps, and gathering information from books, and from the conversations of his father and mother.

Nor was it simply the idea of great armies and bloody battles that stirred his imagination. He had studied the causes of the war, and saw the hideous character of those claims which southern agitators and revolutionists were parading before the civilized world. The institution of slavery stood out before him in all its guilt and enormity, and he seemed perfectly willing to expose himself to any personal danger, or to incur any hazard or loss, if he might help crush this accursed system, and rid the land of his fathers of this foul blot upon her otherwise fair fame.

No doubt there was much that was unnatural and ill-regulated in the fervors of this fierce excitement. His imagination, naturally strong and active, had been unduly developed in the solitude of his life,—in his hours of lonely musing. Yet, after all, there was something grand and heroic in the position of this boy in his far-off home among the hills of Asia. It is of such material that real heroes are made. He would, even then, at so early an age, have " counted all things but loss," if he might personally have been permitted to share in the humblest duties, to bear the lowliest part, in the work of subduing and extirpating the great rebellion.

So matters went on from month to month. With all the rest of the loyal children of America, he felt the agony of the defeat at the first great battle of Bull Run. He shared in all the hopes and high anticipations when McClellan came forward to take the command of the army of the Potomac. He endured the long suspense, the sickening delay and inactivity of the following fall and winter and spring, though he endured them like a young lion shut up in a cage, and beating ineffectually against the bars of his prison.

We are glad, at this point, to introduce a communication from Miss M. A. Proctor, a native of Townsend, Mass., and a graduate of the Normal School at Framingham, but now for several years a most highly valued missionary teacher at Aintab. She gives us a clear and distinct impression of what this boy was, and presents us with a vivid picture of his manner of life before coming to this country.

"I take pleasure in complying with the request of Dr. Schneider, that I would communicate to you some incidents in regard to his son Edward, which may serve to illustrate his boyish life in this country.

"When I became a member of his father's family, in 1859, Eddie was thirteen years of age, — a regular *boy*, bright, vigorous, and active, warm-hearted and impulsive, with much of a boy's restlessness and love of adventure. One could but wonder how so much *boy-life* was to find vent and exercise in this out-of-the-way place, with no school to attend, and not an English-speaking child within a hundred miles for a playmate. Still he usually seemed very happy, and made the house lively with his singing and whistling. He had daily lessons, reciting mostly to his mother, but sometimes to others of the missionary circle. He thought it pretty dull, as most young people would, to study so alone; but he obtained a very good knowledge of Geography, History, and the Natural Sciences: knowledge which is specially needed, and constantly called into use in this land. Arithmetic and Grammar he disliked. Of course, there were many interruptions in such a course of home study, and so he labored under the double disadvantage of being alone, and of being somewhat irregular in his lessons. But the desire to take a good stand when he should enter school in America was a powerful incentive to spur him on.

"Besides his lessons, he had a good deal of work to attend to every day, as the care of his chamber, bringing in wood, and, when he became a little older, the care of the horses.

He had no 'lazy bones,' as the phrase is, and took pleasure in cleaning up the house, or in helping his mother about the cooking. His parents did not like to have him much with the servant, or with the native boys near by; for, however well-disposed many of them might be, yet his very position among them was one of temptation. An American child in his Frank dress naturally *rules* among his playmates, while among older people he is petted and encouraged to say and do smart things.

"Still a boy must have companions, and Eddie often joined a company of school-boys in a walk or at a game of ball. Skating there was none, often not snow enough for coasting more than half-a-dozen days in the course of a winter, although some years we have snow for weeks. But he amused himself with rigging up ships, making flags, pressing and arranging flowers, contriving little gifts for his friends, etc. The two missionary families were in the habit of meeting once a week for dinner and a social evening; and chiefly for Eddie's sake, birthdays, Independence, Christmas and holidays generally were duly observed. In the summer we often went out to the fruit-orchards, and spent a day under the trees, taking our meals in picnic style. These days he enjoyed most thoroughly.

"Eddie did not become a Christian until he went to America. But, carefully as he had been trained, he could but have many serious thoughts. Many times he came to my room, and with tears asked me to pray with him, and tell him what he must do to obtain a new heart. He would seem to be almost ready to give himself up wholly to Christ, and sometimes would say he had done so. Then, as he felt the power of temptation still strong upon him, he would say, ' I never can be a Christian ; this *will* of mine *wont bend ;* ' and for a time he would become careless and indifferent. The last year of his stay with us in Aintab he was more uniform in his serious feelings and desires, and we felt that he would at length be led by the Spirit.

" Edward's patriotism, more than anything else, has made him known and admired, and I wish I could give you a vivid idea of how brightly that flame was burning in his heart while still in this country, and from the very commencement of the war.

"Although born and brought up in Turkey, and having never seen American soil, there was no truer patriot in all New England than our Eddie. He devoured every item of news about the war, waiting as impatiently for our weekly post as any politician for his daily paper, and he was never tired of talking over the battles, etc. It was amusing to see him sit so silently, and sometimes uneasily, while the company were discussing miscellaneous topics, or something pertaining to our missionary work, and to notice how eagerly he would snatch the first opportunity to say, 'Well, what of the *war?* Do you suppose the army of the Potomac has taken Richmond by this time?' McClellan was his great hero for a long time, and he stood up for him after many of his friends had abandoned him; but after a while, he, too, was obliged to let his hero drop.

"He enjoyed committing to memory and reciting patriotic poems, and among these 'Bingen on the Rhine' seemed to be his favorite. He adapted or invented a kind of chant for this, and would chant it by the hour as he sat in his room. In his last letters to friends before joining the army he quoted from it, —

"'Tell my sister not to weep,' etc.

"He often said that if he was in America he would join the army, and was impatient to go home that he might fight for his country. To many this may seem only romance and boyish enthusiasm; but, if it was, there was added to it a devotedness of purpose, and a spirit of self-sacrifice and determination to overcome all obstacles, which enabled him not merely to *dream* of doing, but bravely to carry out his purpose even unto death. He knew, too, more of the realities of army life than any one brought up in New England could do. He had travelled over these rough mule-paths many a day under a burning sun, and also in cold and rain; he had had experience of tent-life, and of the traveller's road-fare, and of sleeping out under the open sky. Boy-like he chose, on those long journeys, to shoulder gun and rough it with the strongest of the company. At one time, when he had got a little in advance of his friends, a party of armed men rode threateningly up to him and demanded who he was. He quietly told them, and they, after satisfying themselves that he was not the person they were in pursuit of, rode off and left him jogging along.

"When he found that his friends were not willing that he should enter the army while so young, he put himself in a way to be ready to when his time should come. He found that mathematics were very important to a naval officer or a tactician; and so, notwithstanding his dislike of figures, we heard of him, scarcely a year after he entered school in America, at Andover, studying arithmetic, algebra, and geometry all at once. Of his various other training processes at Andover you will doubtless hear from his friends.

"Much as Eddie had longed to go to America, it was a hard trial for his affectionate heart when the time came for him to bid all his friends good-by, and leave his father's house. He accompanied us to Aleppo, where the Annual Meeting was to hold its session, and went on from there with the friends from Beirüt. All those last days with us in Aleppo his heart was very full. In the crowded state of the house, he slept on a lounge in the same room with his parents, and hearing his mother got up in the night he called her to him, — 'Mamma, come and let me hug you,' — and so he clung to me as if he could not say the last good-by."

In the foregoing communication, reference is made to the beautiful lines by Mrs. Caroline E. Norton, and both as showing how his thoughts ran, in that distant home, and because they had a meaning for him which he could not then know, and were in some sense prophetic of his own fate, we give two or three stanzas, distinctly to recall them to the reader: —

"A soldier of the Legion lay dying in Algiers;
There was lack of woman's nursing, there was dearth of
    woman's tears;
But a comrade stood beside him, while his life-blood ebbed
    away,
And bent with pitying glances, to hear what he might say.
The dying soldier faltered as he took that comrade's hand,
And he said, 'I never more shall see my own, my native
    land, —
Take a message and a token to some distant friends of mine;
For I was born at Bingen — at Bingen on the Rhine.

"'Tell my brothers and companions, when they meet and
    crowd around,
To hear my mournful story, in the pleasant vineyard ground,

That we fought the battle bravely; and when the day was done
Full many a corse lay ghastly pale beneath the setting sun;
And midst the dead and dying were some grown old in wars,
The death-wounds on their gallant breasts the last of many scars;
But some were young, and suddenly beheld life's morn decline,
And one had come from Bingen — fair Bingen on the Rhine!'

. . . .

"His voice grew faint and hoarse — his grasp was childish weak;
His eyes put on a dying look — he sighed, and ceased to speak;
His comrade bent to lift him, but the spark of life had fled:
The soldier of the Legion in a foreign land was dead!
And the soft moon rose up slowly, and calmly she looked down
On the red sand of the battle-field, with bloody corpses strewn;
Yes, calmly on that dreadful scene her pale light seemed to shine,
As it shone on distant Bingen — fair Bingen on the Rhine."

CHAPTER II.

REMOVAL TO THIS COUNTRY. SCHOOL DAYS.

THE time had at length come when Edward, the youngest of the flock, being now nearly sixteen years of age, was to go to America to receive the advantages of a more perfect education. His early culture had been more broken and neglected than of the other children. The course of events, detailed in the previous chapter, is of itself sufficient to show how irregular must have been his mental training. His life had been one of sudden and strange transitions, leaving little continuous quiet for the acquisition of knowledge or for intellectual discipline.

In the summer of 1862 it was arranged that he, in company with some returning missionaries, should go, for the first time, to the land of his fathers. This, under any circumstances, would have been an event to stir his imagination, and fill his youthful mind with the liveliest anticipations. It was the land of his kindred. It was here that his sisters and brothers were, and the prospect of a reunion with them was most delightful to him. But, above all things, his coming just at that time was made doubly joyful to him because of his intense interest in the fortunes of the war. There was, however, a dark side to the picture, as we have seen from the foregoing letter of Miss Proctor. There was, even then, a kind of forecasting what might happen.

He reached this country in one of the darkest periods of the conflict, — just after the seven-days' battle on the Peninsula, when everything seemed to be going to confusion. The battle of Antietam, however, which soon followed, changed the aspect of the scene and revived the hopes of the loyal people of the land. Nothing would have suited him better than at once to have joined the army of freedom. But he was not yet of military age, and his friends would not consent to his enlisting. After brief visits to his relatives, he went, in the fall of 1862, to Bridgewater, where his brother James was employed as a teacher in the Normal School; and was there placed at school under the general direction and care of his brother.

Now let it be understood that, in briefly delineating the early years of this boy, we have by no means intended to hold him up as a model child. Far enough from this. His qualities were quite unlike those of his elder brother James, and such as excite far greater fear and anxiety in parents as to what the result may be. His was one of those natures that is likely to turn strongly either toward good or evil, and one often waits tremblingly to see which direction will be taken. Many a child, with the same essential qualities, has become an early wreck. The victims of intemperance are often these children of high and generous natures, noble impulses, who are early led astray; and, when once they are on the downward path, go from bad to worse with a strange rapidity. But here was a child of many prayers. Around him had been thrown the restraining influences of religion from his early years. And, as we have already seen, before he came to this country, he had deeply felt his need of the renewing grace of God, and had sought, as he thought, earnestly that he might be owned and accepted as a child. But those feelings had been evanescent. In the judgment of charity, there was no good reason to suppose, at the time of his coming to this country, that he knew what true and genuine religion was.

After reaching Bridgewater, he occasioned his brother no little anxiety because of a certain waywardness,— a facility in yielding to evil companionships. James felt a heavy burden of responsibility in the case, and labored and prayed that this young brother might be guided to the "Lamb of God that taketh away the sin of the world." And his prayers and labors were not in vain. In the spring and early summer of 1863 there was a prevailing religious interest in Bridgewater. Edward's heart was deeply moved, and he came forward, and as he believed, and as others about him believed, made a full consecration of himself to Christ.

June 12th he writes to his sister Eliza:—

"Dear Lizzie,— I thought, as I felt so happy, I would make you happy. . . I hope I have found Christ. Oh, a blessed thought that is! Yesterday, as I was walking out alone, I was looking at the clouds and saw something beautiful. I thought I saw a beautiful golden palace, shining and glistening in the sun; and Jesus was beckoning to me and pointing to it. All this may have been fancy. Whether imagination or not, it looked beautiful. I feel happy. The world has a brighter look to me now than it ever had before, and it is my duty to go to the war. I trust I am ready to to die, and am ready to go as soon as it is best for me."

This letter was detained until the next day, and he adds:—

"Saturday Morning.

"This morning I went to the prayer-meeting, and I got up and told them that I wanted to be a Christian, and asked them to pray for me. Oh, I felt so happy! I enjoyed the meeting so much! It was very hard at first to take this step; but I made up my mind to do it, and have done it. Lizzie dear, wont you pray for me? I need the prayers of Christians very much."

Under date of June 20th, he writes to his

father: — "I suppose that it will gladden your heart, if I should tell you that I am a Christian. Yes, since I wrote you last, I rejoice in the hope that I am a Christian. Everything has a brighter look. I am now ready to die at any moment, I hope, and if it is my duty to join the army, you cannot now have any objection, can you? I don't say that it is my duty to go now, but the time is coming, and it is not very far off, I think."

On the same day James writes to his father: — "I have time to write you only a few lines, but that will be better than nothing. Eddie has told you the best piece of news, — that he rejoices in the new birth. I believe he is sincere. His whole life and conduct are altered. I can hardly believe it, but it comes in direct answer to prayer. You have prayed, and mother prayed, and others have prayed. I presented his case as a petitioner at one of our morning prayer-meetings, and earnest prayers indeed were offered, and I believe God answered them."

We must now go back a little in our narrative, in order that certain things, which will follow, may be clearly understood. It has been explained in the early part of this volume, that the present Mrs. Schneider, who went out to Aintab in 1858, returned to this country to make a brief visit, especially on account of her aged mother, landing in Boston in the month of May, 1863. When references, therefore, are made to her, for some months to come, it will be understood that she was in this country. Her mother was in Carbondale, Pa., in the family of a grandson, Rev. Henry Abbott, an Episcopal clergyman. So soon as Edward hears of his mother's arrival, he writes to her, under date of May 14th, 1863 : — "My dearest mother, oh, how glad I am to hear you are in Boston, only twenty-seven miles from me! I can hardly realize it. Can it be true that you are in America? Next week on Friday my vacation comes, and I can see you. James proposes that I should spend it with you in Saxonville. It is only a week long; would you be willing to defer your visit to Carbondale a few days on my account? I hope you will, — I almost know you will. Next week, on Thursday, our school has an examination. I dread it a little, but will try to do my best, and go through it bravely like a soldier."

Mrs. Schneider, after a brief delay in New England, went to Carbondale, Pa., to her mother, and there she remained closely until her mother's death, which occurred about the first of August.

June 27th Edward writes from Bridgewater to his sister Eliza: —

"Dear Sister Lizzie, — Just one hour ago I received your letter, and I came to the sublime conclusion to answer it right off. You are a jewel of a darling of a sister to write to me so soon, and I thank you very much for your letter. . . You wish to know how I am getting along. Well, this past week has not been a very pleasant one. My lessons went wrong . . and then I have had the thought that I am not 'a soldier of the Cross,' and have had fears that my love to Jesus was growing cold; so you see it has been a dismal week to me. What can I do? I pray to God to help me; but my prayers are not earnest enough. And then again, James has spoken to me about taking a part in meetings; but what can I say? I don't know what to say, and I don't think I can pray, yet, before other people. I could

not say anything. What shall I do? Please,
when you write me next, tell me."

In July he sends the following letter to his
mother: —

"BRIDGEWATER, July 11, 1863.

"DEAR AUNT SUSIE, — Please to excuse my
tardiness in answering your note, but I have
been very busy. I have very little time to
myself. Since I heard from you, you have
had a terrible battle fought near you, — I mean
that of Gettysburg. How I wish I could have
been there! I mean by that, I wish I could
have been there to fight.

"What are father's views about my going to
the war? Would he be willing to have me go
now that his native State has been invaded?
. . I want so much to fight for my country.
I can't stay much longer. I *must* go. I feel
it my duty to go. I don't want to go for the
fun of being a soldier, or for bounty money,
but to fight. I have got to die sometime, and
if I go and get killed, and go to heaven, and
be with my mother and sister, I would go to-
day. . . I want to enlist in six weeks; may
I not? Oh, give me the privilege of suffering

for my country! I want to enlist in some New York regiment, cavalry or infantry. I hope I will not be disappointed.

"In two weeks James's school will be through, and we both are coming down to Englewood, in two weeks and a half. . . When are you coming to Englewood? Wont you be there when James and I are there? I want to see you very much. I am not at all satisfied with the glimpse I got of you at Saxonville.

"Since I wrote you last I have at times doubted whether I am a true Christian. I find it very hard to do right always. James says that I ought to take part in meetings. How can I? I don't know what to say. This troubles me a good deal. Will you pray for me that I may be guided aright? . . . Please write me soon, if possible before I go to Englewood.

"Yours affectionately,
"NED."

On the 12th of August James writes to his mother, still at Carbondale:— "We boys want to see you, as much as you want to see us. We will be in Saxonville sometime on Tuesday next (a week from to-day). I will write to Mrs. Northrop and ask her if it is convenient to her to have us come. Eddie has changed wonderfully. He is a very good boy."

His desire to enter the army never left him. Whatever other subject might be omitted in his letters, this was sure to have a place somewhere. He writes to his sister Eliza from Framingham, August 27th, —

"DEAR LIZZIE, — I left Englewood in high hopes, but everything has changed in regard to my going to the war; and next week I shall be established at school in Andover. It has been and is a great disappointment to me that I can't go into the army; but it is all for the best that I don't go, I suppose, though it is hard to be disappointed. I shall go to Andover, and try to do my duty, and study hard."

Accordingly, in the early fall of 1863, he went from the school in Bridgewater to Andover, where he entered Phillips Academy. His one year in this country, with the mental discipline it had afforded, with the advantages derived from the faithful care and influence of his brother, and, more especially, under the convicting and regenerating influences of the Holy Spirit, had made him another person, — had given him more enlarged and sober ideas of life. But, in the midst of all these changes, his intense desire to enter the army and fight for his country had not in the least abated, but rather increased.

To show still farther the strength of this feeling in him, — how powerfully this desire to be a soldier had taken hold upon his thoughts, — we will copy, almost at random, a few extracts from his letters written to various persons during his school-days.

From Bridgewater, June 9th, 1863, he writes: — " What do you think of the war? Are you any more willing that I should be a soldier-boy now than you were last July? I have not given up the idea, and I hope I shall not. . . You may perhaps laugh at me, if I tell you that I feel it my duty to go. Yes, I feel it more and more."

March 20th he writes from the same place: —" I try to bear all without complaining; for a soldier *must* bear without complaining. I don't mean to say I am one yet, but when I am one, I shall have to bear pain, fatigue and hunger: so, you see, I am getting ready to be a soldier. I receive hardly any sympathy from my friends in my military plans. Oh! I want to go now, and fight for our glorious starry banner!"

April 24th again he writes: — " I was feeling badly all last week, because I saw no prospect of my being a soldier, or obtaining a military education; but after a week's suffering, I have determined to wait patiently till my time comes. Meanwhile, I will try to get a good practical English education."

In the following August his hopes of being permitted to enlist were raised very high, and he thought, for a time, that he should certainly go into the army. August 29th he writes from Saxonville, where he is spending his vacation: — " What can I do? I did all in my power to go, and tried every means that I had; but it was of no use; it was decreed from on high that I should not go, and what good will it do for me to murmur? I must bear my disappointment without murmuring. I try not to complain. . . It is decided that I shall go to Andover to school. I go with the determination to study hard, — yes, hard as I can, and try to do my duty both to God and man."

The following passage is of different character. He had received a present from his brother James, then at Ship Island, and in writing to a dear friend he says: — "I have not been grateful to James for his kindness to me. He has done a great deal for me, and, now that he is away, I begin more and more to realize it. His influence over me has done me a vast deal of good. I hope you wont think I am trying to make myself out to be so very good now. No; far from it. I mean that, had it not been for James, I would not be where I am now."

The following are extracts from his letters to his sister Eliza, written at Andover during the fall term of 1863: —

"Sunday Evening.

"I have just been to a prayer-meeting among the students. Oh, it was a blessed season! There were over sixty present, and Jesus was there with us. If you could have heard the prayers it would have done your heart good. When I went there I thought I would not take part in the meeting, but after

I had been there a little while, I felt it my duty to speak, and I did speak, and how happy I felt afterwards! I feel happy now, for I feel as if I had done a little for Jesus. I have now come out for Jesus, and I must and will work for him."

Again he writes: — " Yesterday evening, I went to the class prayer-meeting. Many got up and spoke, and among them two that had been converted during the past week. There is a revival going on in our school. Many are inquiring 'What shall I do to be saved?' The prayer-meetings are very interesting. I enjoy them very much."

November 4th, 1863, he writes his sister: —

"Dear Lizzie, — I have a little spare time this afternoon, and I have sat down, pen in hand, to have a little chat with you.

"I expected to see you at James' ordination at Bridgewater, and was very much disappointed not to see you there. . . As I write, the sun is sinking gradually in the west. I wonder what you and A—— are doing just now while I am writing. I wonder what Willie is doing: perchance sweating down in the engine-room. I wonder also what James is doing: perhaps teaching his soldiers how to read, or telling his men of the love of Jesus to those who will serve him. Yes, I wonder if you are thinking of me as I am thinking of you.

"To-day I have had to read a composition (subject, 'Malta'), and have had to speak a piece; and next Thursday I will have to deliver something like an essay before the 'Society of Inquiry,' of which I am a member. Just think of my giving an essay? Well, it must be so, and I can't get out of it. . . .

"So, good-night.

"BROTHER EDWARD."

In December, 1863, he makes another earnest appeal to his father for liberty to go the war. He writes from Englewood, where he is spending his vacation: —

"December 1, 1863.

"DEAR FATHER, — It is vacation now, and I am spending it with Lizzie and A——. I received your kind letter a week before school closed, and it did me a great deal of good. I should have written you before the term closed; but you can hardly realize how busy I am from morning to night, and from one end of the week to the other. The time passes very rapidly. I have been at Andover one term of *twelve* weeks, and expect to be there two terms more of *fifteen* weeks, which will bring me near, if not to, August of next year.

"It was a great disappointment to me not to go to the army, but I clearly saw God had designed that I should not go at present. I can't as yet see the reason why I was not permitted by Providence to be a soldier; but I know that it is all for the best. . . I shall wait till I am eighteen patiently and diligently. I will study, and then, if it is my duty to go, I shall shoulder my musket and march to the music of the Union, with a determined purpose. . . I shall try next term to get the highest mark in the English department of our school. This term the highest mark given in our department was 7.73 (8 is perfect). I got 7.55, which you see is only eighteen hundredths less than the best scholar. . . .

"Yours,
"EDWARD."

When we remember how intense and long

continued in him had been this interest in the war,— how constantly this feeling makes itself manifest under all circumstances and on all occasions, — we cannot but regard this devotion to scholarship at the same time, this ambition to excel, as indicative of somewhat remarkable powers of concentration and self-control. And, especially, when we take into view the fact that hitherto he has not been trained to continuous and systematic habits of study, his present devotion to books is, to say the least, highly commendable. During the May term, which had just closed, he had also been subject to the excitement arising from his brother's enlistment and departure to join the army. In the letter to his father, from which we have just quoted, he says: — " You perhaps know that James, instead of being adjutant of his regiment, is the chaplain. He was ordained at Bridgewater five weeks ago to-day. The regiment came on to New York last Wednesday, and sailed for New Orleans . . . the next day (it being Thanksgiving). James's regiment is to be in Gen. Banks' department, and may possibly be ordered off to join our army in Texas."

In the midst of his chronic war excitement, with these disturbing causes superadded, it certainly argues well for the character of the boy that he should thus earnestly and quietly pursue his studies and attain so high a grade of scholarship. Indeed, it is very evident as we look back over the course of events, that he was acting under higher and more commanding motives than those which ruled him when he first landed on our shores. The brief sentence already quoted from James's letter, namely, " Edward has changed wonderfully; he is a very good boy now," means a great deal. In the short space of one year, he seems to have passed from the impulsive, half-unreasoning state of a boy, and reached the collected force and discretion of a man.

At the close of the vacation he went back to Andover and entered with vigor upon the winter term. But he never gave up the idea of being a soldier. The following letter, written February 1st, 1864, will show with what strength this idea had taken hold of him, and how constantly it followed him through all the changes of his life in this country : —

"Dear Lizzie,—To-day the President called for 500,000 more men. You will have seen it long before this reaches you. What shall I do?

"The boys here in the school are awaking to a sense of their duty to their country. I think many of my school-mates will go, and among them are my best friends and companions. . . Don't you think it is my duty to go now, after this last call for troops? I am sure, if ever it was my duty to go, it is now, for now is the time when our country needs the men.

"Do you think that I must wait till I hear from James before I enlist, or not? The fact is, Lizzie, it will be nearly two months before I can get an answer from him. Do you think it would be justifiable in me to enlist before I heard from him? I am inclined to think that it would, for, in his last letter, he said that he was glad father had given his consent to my going to the war. I do so want to go with my friends! Why, it will make me crazy to have my school-mates, class-mates, and best friends here go, and I have to stay. Oh, no, I can't do so! I must go. I am not excited. I write calmly. . . . Don't you think I had better go? How can you or any one hold me back, when

I ought to go by all means? It is too bad to trouble you so much about my affairs, but if it were not for your and A——'s sake, I would not hesitate one moment in going.

"Now I feel I must go, and it will be unjust to keep me from going. I shall write to James to-night and ask his consent; but most likely he will not get it for three weeks. I say again, I *must* go and serve my country. I don't think I will have to serve long, for the war will not last more than a year longer. Please write soon and tell me what you think I had better do; for on the 10th of March they will draft, and I want to enlist before that. Write soon.

"Your affectionate brother.

"Edward."

His prophecy, at last, draws near the fulfilment. The reader will remember what he wrote to his father the previous summer: "I don't say that it is my duty to go now, but the time is coming, and it is not very far off, I think."

Mrs. Schneider, after a brief visit to her native land, — after being providentially permitted to minister to the last days of her aged and widowed mother, — set out on her return to Aintab in the early part of 1864. She went back by way of England; and Dr. Schneider, who was desired to spend a short time in England in labors in behalf of the Turkish Aid Society, met her there. From her he learned more fully all that had been passing in regard to the dear boys in America, and it was at that time that he gave his consent that Edward should enter the army. There is, perhaps, no better place than this to introduce the following touching passage from the letter of Dr. S. to the writer, giving an account of this matter. After going rapidly over the items of early personal history, which we have already recorded, he says: —

"It will thus be seen that he was early thrown on his own resources, — being very much alone and without the superintending care of his parents. This circumstance may have had a marked influence in developing the decided spirit of a true soldier, which he afterwards exhibited. . . . From the commencement of the war in America, even before he had reached its shores, he felt a very deep interest in its progress. He was well posted in its history, and could give the particulars of many important events and phases of the rebellion. All that he read about it only increased his desire to aid in crushing it. After reaching America this desire constantly increased. He asked permission to enter the army. But as he was not yet eighteen years of age, and, when he first arrived in America, was not yet hopefully pious, I did not feel that it was his duty to enlist. I became very anxious on this point, as his desire to participate in the war was constantly and rapidly growing. My earnest prayer was, for a long time, that if the Lord would only give him a new heart, I could then consent to his going to the war, or to any part of the globe to which He might call him. This was the burden of my prayer for months. I could not think of his going to the war without a good hope; and yet his desire to enlist became irresistibly strong. When this prayer was finally answered in his hopeful conversion, I could no longer refuse my consent. Accordingly, when, some months after he had expressed a hope as a Christian, he again earnestly pleaded to be permitted to enlist, I could no longer refuse assent. I well remember the circumstances surrounding me, and the feelings with which I consented. In Dublin (being at that time on a visit to England), in the third story of our kind host, I sat down, and gave my written permission to his entering the army; but it was with the decided presentiment that the result would be fatal to the dear boy. But as I had promised the Lord that, if he would only give him a renewed heart, I would consent to his being employed in any service or sent to any part of the habitable globe, I could not do otherwise, whatever might be the issue. I felt sure the Judge of all the earth would do right, whether the lad should be spared to return to us after the war had ceased, as so many have done, or be sacrificed to the well-being of his country. . . .

"When he finally became a soldier he seemed very happy and contented, feeling, as I believe, that he was in the path of duty. And though he knew the dangers to which he was exposed, as he considered himself in the path of duty, he seemed to be perfectly satisfied with his position as a soldier."

March 5th, 1864, Chaplain Schneider writes to his father from Key West, as follows: — "I gave my consent finally to Eddie's enlisting. You have given your consent. . . As he has been very often disappointed, and has borne the disappointment quite well, and is a *good* boy, and has just received the strengthening influences of a revival at Andover, and as this is probably the last opportunity he will have to enlist, I cheerfully gave my consent to his going. . . He has very much improved in writing. He has done well at Andover."

CHAPTER III.

ENTERS THE ARMY. EARLY EXPERIENCES.

NO sooner had the consent of his friends been obtained, than Edward sprang forward like an imprisoned bird let loose from a cage.* All along he had evidently believed the time was soon coming, and now indeed it had come. He had been preparing for this for months. During the latter part of his connection with Phillips Academy, he had slept upon the bare floor, that he might learn " to endure hardness as a good soldier." He

---

* About the time of his enlistment he called upon a family in Boston, where he was well acquainted, and seemed running over with joy that the consent of his friends had been gained, so that he could go into the army. Alluding to this subject, and using the common designation of the boys at Phillips Academy for their respected principal, he said: "If Mr. Taylor makes any objection, I shall tell him that I am now going into the service of a greater 'Uncle Sam' than he is."

maintained that self-control, of which we have spoken in the previous chapter, to the last of his stay in the Academy. Eager as he was to go, yet, while he remained, he applied himself diligently to books, and gained the high approbation of his teachers.

February 9th, 1864, James, then with his regiment at Ship Island, writes his father: — "I hear very gratifying and cheering accounts of Eddie. He is developing *well.*"

He enlisted in the early part of March. One of the regiments then forming in Massachusetts was the 57th, under the command of Colonel William F. Bartlett, of Boston. Company K, of this regiment, to which young Schneider attached himself, was a company of sharpshooters, to be armed with the Spencer rifle. The head-quarters of the regiment, before being mustered into service, were at Worcester. This was among the last regular regiments enrolled in Massachusetts, the highest number being the 62d, and that numbered as the 60th being only a regiment of one hundred days' men. The soldiers composing the 57th were not drawn from any one particular locality, as in the case of many of the earlier regiments, but they came together indiscriminately from all parts of the State. It was forming in the fall of 1863 and in the winter and early spring of 1864, in bad weather, and its accommodations at Worcester were not of the best. After enlisting, and before going permanently into camp, he paid a last visit to Englewood. His brother, Rev. William B. Dwight, in a letter written at a later date, describes this visit, and the impression made on his own mind by Eddie's conversation and manner: —

"He was unmistakably a Christian. I can testify to the great change which he had undergone since he indulged a hope in Christ. And in taking his country's uniform, and putting his life in peril, I believe he was actuated by the noblest principle. On previous occasions he may have looked at the *romance* of the thing, but he evidently took no such view of it when he was here on his last visit. I was then very much struck by his sedateness and manliness. He said very little about the army, but conversed mostly about such topics of love and friendship as would naturally engross the mind of one who felt the premonition that he

ENTERS THE ARMY. 291

should never return. He was in the best of spirits, however, and felt that he was doing his duty; and we all think that he was. He laid all his plans with much thoughtfulness, and made every preparation to enable him to perform well the arduous duties of the field. Among other things, I will mention, that, just before he left, we ascertained that, during the whole of his last term at Andover, he had slept every night on nothing softer than the floor, to enable him to meet the hardships of the camp. He bid us an affectionate good-by, and went into camp at Worcester. Here, as the company was not yet mustered in, he had to put up for weeks with very poor accommodations and very wretched fare."

This passage sets the young soldier very clearly before us, and we see that the frivolity of the boy has gone, and the soberness and dignity of young manhood have taken its place.

March 23d, 1864, Edward writes from camp Wool, at Worcester, to A——: — "How kind it was in you to write to me! I thank you ever so much. I received it, together with Eliza's last letter, yesterday, — they having been here one whole day without my knowledge. . . It is a blustering, cold day, to-day; in fact it is very cold. I must thank you again and again for the nice warm stockings you knit for me. I don't know how I would have got along without that pair, for we have not been furnished with stockings by the government. There are nearly thirty of our company in camp, and some are coming in daily. We are quartered with another company, but as soon as there is a sufficient number (I can't say how many) we will have quarters by ourselves. That will be so much better. Our company will be the crack company of the regiment, — that is, they are trying to have it so. Every effort is being made to have all Americans, and no Irishmen. The part of the company that is in camp is composed of nice young men, though some are older. There are several that I like very much. There seems to exist a sort of brotherhood among the sharpshooters. . . Of the barracks we are quartered in now, I can say but little. There are large cracks, through which the cold air comes in at a great rate. We suffer a great deal from the cold and from various other causes. But I would not have you think, for a moment, I am sorry that I enlisted. *I am glad* that I enlisted, and have not for a moment been sorry."

Again, March 30th, he writes to the same: — "It is a rough day to-day. It snows, it hails, and the wind sweeps across our camp like fury. We have two stoves in our barrack, but one of them smokes when the wind blows, and makes us very uncomfortable. But this is not all. Our barrack was built of green lumber, and, when it dried, it shrunk up, causing large cracks all over the building, through which the cold comes in at a great rate. I could go on and describe everything around me, by which you would infer that we are not very comfortably quartered; but it will not do any good, and, above all, I *don't* wish to complain. We shall have better quarters when our company is mustered in and organized; but when that will be, I cannot now say. Our company looks more hopeful since I wrote last. By the end of this week there will be fifty or sixty in camp. The fact is, more than that number have enlisted, but they are slow in coming into camp."

April 10th, he writes: — "Last week was one of the busiest, as well as the happiest since

I arrived in camp. To my great joy, we were mustered into the national service as the tenth company (Sharpshooters) 57th Massachusetts Regiment of Infantry. Our company numbers ninety strong, and there are more for it in camp. . . . It is snowing again, which makes the camp look desolate; but I don't care much, — we are happy inside. The weather is not so cold as it has been. During those cold days we suffered a little, I guess. But never mind, I feel rough and ready for any emergency. . . It is a great disappointment to me not to see you again; but it can't be helped though; there is a very slight chance of my getting on."

The regiment was mustered into the service of the United States April 6th, 1864, and on the 18th of April it left the State to be moved forward to the seat of war. It was not full at the time it was ordered to move. It numbered at that time about nine hundred and fifty men. But serious work was in prospect, and all available men must be brought forward to the front. Young Schneider had been longing, for years, for an opportunity to serve his country, and when the occasion came, it came in earnest. There was the widest diversity during the progress of the war, in the fortunes of regiments, in respect to actual fighting. Some regiments would go forward to the front, and remain in a drilling and seasoning process for months without a touch of real fighting. Others were taken fresh from the recruiting camp, and plunged at once into some of the most terrible battles of the war. Many will remember the circumstances connected with the 35th Massachusetts Regiment, Col. Edward A. Wild commanding, in 1862. This regiment left Massachusetts August 22d of that year, and arrived upon the ground just in season to be at once moved forward with the troops concentrating for the battle of Antietam, which was fought on the 17th of September. In this great battle, the 35th, utterly unused to such scenes, was exposed to a most terrific fire from the enemy, and was very badly cut up.

It fared somewhat so with young Schneider's regiment, the 57th. Gen. Grant was getting ready for that great fighting and flanking movement, by which he was to make his way to Richmond, and men were pushed forward with all haste, and by forced marches, from every direction.

Rev. Mr. Dwight, in the letter from which we have already quoted, describes the toils which the regiment went through as soon as ever it arrived from Massachusetts. " They went to Annapolis, and were immediately marched to Washington, on *two* very hot days, a distance of sixty miles, which for the first march was terrible." From Washington, the regiment passed out of sight, with the rest of the gathering host, and men, everywhere, understood that something was to be done, though they knew not exactly what. - For a few days there was anxious suspense throughout the land, and then came the news of the battle of the " Wilderness." At first, men doubted whether it was to be called a victory or a defeat. People had grown used to those great battles just across the Potomac, which were first heralded as victories, and afterwards turned out to be something quite different; and from long experience they had learned not now to indulge in a hasty and inconsiderate joy. It was known that the losses on our side had been very great, and it would not have been a matter of special surprise, if the loyal army, as in previous campaigns, had found it best — all for strategic purposes, of course — to have fallen back a little, and taken up a position somewhat nearer Washington. A few days pass away, — days of sore anxiety, — and then we find terrific fighting going on at Spotsylvania Court House. Men study their maps, and discover that this at least is not a retreat, though the enemy may try to give out that they are seeking to draw our army into a position where it may be overwhelmed. But, on the day after this last-named battle, comes back that ringing word from Gen. Grant, "*I propose to fight it out on this line, if it takes all summer.*" And then the country began to breathe freer; for they found that a real man was at the head, and not the man who was called general-in-chief when the seven days' battles on the Peninsula were fought.

But here was this 57th Regiment, only seventeen days after they broke camp at Worcester, in one of the most terrible and desperately-fought battles of the war, and destined to share in others in quick succession for a month and more to come. The boy, only seventeen years old, who, but a little more than two months ago, was reciting his lessons in Phillips Academy, is now passing through a campaign, which, for toil and fighting, might well appal the veteran, after years of discipline and experience in the field. Says Rev. W. B. Dwight, speaking of this campaign which began at the Wilderness and ended with Petersburg: —" Words cannot describe its suffering. I have seen many of the soldiers who have been through it, and they look as if they had been steeped in the rays of the mid-day sun, and then scathed by lightning. They commenced with the terrible battle of the Wilderness, and marched and countermarched, and fought incessantly for *five* weeks, when Burnside's corps (in which was the 57th Massachusetts) had its severest fight on the banks of the North Anna. After that was over, out of nine hundred and fifty, who composed the regiment five weeks before, only one hundred were left capable of bearing arms. Eddie himself was wounded in the leg and taken to the hospital. We received a letter from him, in the hospital, mentioning his sufferings, but not complaining of them; speaking of his wound as slight, and manifesting the best of spirits. He had an opportunity to go to hospital at Washington and recruit; but he insisted on rejoining the regiment, and we received a letter from him at Hanover town. He had been in two more fights. He had then been two whole days without any food, and had been fighting most of the time; but he said they were expecting food hourly. He still wrote in good spirits, — no complaining whatever."

Perhaps we can in no way give a more graphic idea of the immense proportions and severe toils and dangers of this campaign, than by copying a brief record of it, day by day, as it stands in the " Chronological History of the Great Rebellion," prepared for " Johnson's New Illustrated Atlas" : —

May 5th. — " First day of the great battle of the Wilderness. Gen. Grant began to move toward forming a line faced westward, and advancing toward Lee; who, to begin with, attacked Grant on the march, aiming to crush his right centre, or to get between his right and the Rapidan. This attack was vigorously repulsed. Lee then (at 3 P. M.) tried to break in between our centre under Warren and left under Hancock, and nearly succeeded ; but was at last repulsed by an advance along our whole line ; and at nightfall the fight was indecisive, and loss heavy on both sides ; but Grant's force was in far better position for further fighting than in the morning."

May 6th. — " Second day of the battle of the Wilderness. Both leaders meant to attack ; but Lee was about fifteen minutes ahead, and attacked with tremendous fury all day, beginning before 5 A. M., trying our right, left, and centre, one after another, and most frequently gaining a temporary advantage, but only to be repulsed by our troops. The final attack of the day upon our right came near being a very damaging affair ; but our troops were rallied by Gen. John Sedgwick, with unsparing personal exertion and exposure, and the army saved. In the battles of this and the preceding day, each side lost, probably fifteen thousand all told. . . The result was, however, that Gen. Grant held his ground, and at the end of his second day's fight pursued his plan of advancing on Richmond by a move on Spotsylvania Court House."

May 8th. — " Severe fighting before Spotsylvania Court House; our troops carry a rebel position, but only after heavy loss. The day resulted in our taking position within two miles of the Court House, Lee's army holding a line a mile in our front, very strongly placed and intrenched. Hancock and Burnside to-day encamp twenty miles away from the Wilderness battle-field."

May 10th. — " First day's battle at Spotsylvania Court House. After heavy cannonade, — artillery being used for the first time since Grant advanced, — there was skirmishing until noon, then an obstinate attack by our troops without success; skirmishing again, and at the end of the day another attack by our whole line, in which Upton's brigade stormed the rebel works, and took one thousand prisoners and several guns, but had to retreat, bringing them off. Day's work indecisive, and loss tremendous, — probably ten thousand on each side."

May 12th. — " Grant's second corps, under Hancock, charges the left of the rebel works in a fog, at dawn, with the bayonet, and hardly firing a gun; surprises at breakfast and captures within an hour a whole division,— men, officers, Brig. Gen. G. H. Stewart, and Maj. General E. Johnson commanding, with thirty guns. Hancock instantly charged and took the rebel second line also. This splendid dash giving us a key-point to the rebel entrenchments, the rest of the day was used in furious rebel assaults (no less than five in all) to regain their lost ground, and furious Union assaults to gain more, but with no further decisive advantage on either side. Loss, on each side, about ten thousand in all."

May 14th.— "Grant had prepared during last night for another flank attack on the rebel right; but the mud and rain last night had made the ground this morning totally impassable. Both sides intrenching."

May 15th.— "The first day of rest for the Army of the Potomac for fifteen days."

May 18th.— "Fierce and obstinate attacks on Lee's lines before Spotsylvania Court House; but they were found totally impregnable, and our troops withdrawn after heavy loss."

May 21st.— "Grant's whole army leaves

Spotsylvania Court House, continuing its flanking movement towards Hanover Court House, Lee having already gone. Some skirmishing along our rear."

May 23d. — " Grant's army reaches and crosses the North Anna. Hancock's and Warren's corps are violently resisted, but drive the rebels and make good their positions across the river. Sheridan with his cavalry leaves White House to rejoin Grant."

May 24th. — " Grant completes the crossing of the North Anna."

May 27th. — " Grant's advance reaches Hanover town, on the Pamunkey, about fifteen miles north-east from Richmond, and new supply-base made at White House. Lee evacuates his line on the South Anna, and moves round again to face Grant."

June 1st. — " Battle at Cold Harbor, first day. Severe fighting all day, and our forces hold the position at Cold Harbor in spite of the furious and obstinate assaults of the enemy. We also carry and take part of the rebel rifle-pits; yet the advantages are not decisive."

June 2d. — " Skirmishing all day between Grant and Lee, and a rebel charge on the 5th and 9th corps, in the afternoon, while changing position, which was repulsed with loss, after heavy fighting."

June 3d. — " Third day's fighting at Cold Harbor, being the principal battle. Grant attacked Lee's lines in force, carried the outer works in two places; but the troops were driven back, though they intrenched and held their ground within fifty yards of the enemy. A furious rebel attack, at 8 P. M., was repulsed with heavy loss."

June 4th. — " Grant's forces intrenching. At 9 P. M. violent attack by rebels on Hancock's, Wright's, and Smith's corps; repulsed, however, with rebel loss of over three hundred killed, and one thousand wounded and prisoners."

June 5th. — " Second rebel night attack; directed against Hancock's troops. Rebels retreat, after an hour's severe fighting, with serious loss."

June 12th. — " This afternoon the Army of the Potomac begins to move to cross the James. In the night, the 6th and 9th corps cross the Chickahominy to Charles City Court House; the 2d and 5th moving towards Wilcox's wharf, and the 18th corps going to White House to take transports."

June 15th. — "The crossing of the James by Grant's army completed; the whole force having been drawn out from within fifty yards of the enemy's intrenchments, and moved fifty-five miles by the flank, carried across the Chickahominy and James, — the latter two thousand feet wide and eighty-four feet deep,— with a whole loss by skirmishing and straggling of not over four hundred."

This is the kind of life which the missionary boy from Aintab — the young student from Phillips Academy — lived for five successive weeks, at the very opening of his military career. Surely, his longing to do something to help his country and crush the rebellion was speedily and abundantly gratified. There are not many military campaigns on record more exhausting than this; yet the boy goes through, in spite of his wound, and is at length with the army before Petersburg. The 57th Regiment, for services there performed, was entitled to inscribe on its banners, *Wilderness*, *Spotsylvania*, *North Anna*, and *Cold Harbor*, which were no slight affairs, but tremendous and furious battles, lasting, each, two or three days.

It happened, as a somewhat noticeable fact, that the news of James's death at Key West reached Englewood May 5th, the day on which the great battle of the Wilderness began. Precisely when this news reached Edward, we have not the means of knowing. But it was not probably many days after, that he was made acquainted with the sad intelligence, and he marched and fought all the way to Petersburg with this thought of his brother's death and the grief of the scattered members of his household lying like a heavy burden upon his heart. The sadness of this death, in its relations to dear A———, he had pondered all over in those busy days of toil and fighting, and he had solemnly adopted her as a sister beloved, who should be watched over with fraternal care. He would help her, so far as was in his power, to bear the burden which had fallen so heavily upon her.

A few brief extracts from his letters during this memorable campaign, written in snatches of time, and mostly in pencil, to his sister Eliza and dear A———, will appropriately close this chapter.

On the 11th of May, dating his letter, " On the Road to Richmond," but being near Spotssylvania Court House, he says:—" I have a moment's time to write. I am, as yet, well,— safe and sound. Yesterday afternoon the shot and shell flew around us quite lively. Our company is detached from the regiment, supporting the 7th Maine Battery; and yesterday, when the rebs came out of the woods and charged on our lines, we had to work spry, helping the battery boys.

" I was hardly in any danger in the nine-mile Wilderness battle. . . I have not been hurt yet in this battle, but may be before we get through. Our plan now is to march and fight and drive the rebels. At the battle of the Wilderness, our regiment lost three hundred in killed, wounded, and missing. We lost three from our company."

In another letter, written May 15th, he goes back, and gives a rapid account of their long marches before the battle of the Wilderness, and of the part taken in that battle by his regiment. On the first day, which was the most destructive day for his regiment, his company was detached for other service. But on the

second day, after Colonel Bartlett was himself wounded, the company rejoined the regiment. When this letter was written, on the 15th, he does not appear to have heard of James's death. But in another letter, soon after, but whose date we cannot quite make out, he says:—
"O Lizzie! what *sad, sad* news from James! It was like a thunder-bolt to me. I feel as if I had lost a father in him. Now I must depend upon myself, and act out an independent course. Would that I could sit down by you, and mingle my tears with yours! I love A—— the more, and shall try to be more of a protector. James gave his sword and belt and sash and revolver to me [this was after James took the office of chaplain], you remember; and if his things are sent home, will you keep them for me? I wish to keep them as his last present to me."

June 2d he writes to dear A——:

"I have not written you for a month to-day, neither have I had a letter from you since then. This month, which has just passed, has been one of the most eventful ones of my life, having passed through a great deal: hard, long marches, — been almost starved at times. I have passed through four battles or engagements; but in the last one I had the fortune or misfortune to receive a rebel compliment in shape of a spent musket-ball in the left foot, causing thereby a slight wound, but enough to disable me for a week or more; at the end of which time I reported back to my regiment for duty. I had a chance to go to Washington to a hospital; that is, I could have got there by sneaking. But no; I wanted to be with our regiment when we take Richmond. I am not well yet, but will be very soon. After I was wounded (at the battle of North Anna River), I lay in the woods one day and night before I could be taken care of. The agents of the U. S. Christian Commission have been very kind to me. They gave me a dinner, consisting of two pieces of ham, some apple-sauce, and two soft crackers. This was a dinner better than I have had for months. (We have lived on hard-tack, salt pork, fresh beef, coffee, and sugar, entirely since we left Worcester.) I assure you it tasted good.

"I have been feeling sad for the last few days, for I have lost a brother who was to me more than a brother, and deeply do I sympathize with you in your bereavement. . . . I love you as a sister, and will do all in my power for you. O A——! do write me often, if you can, for I need letters more than ever, for we are having hard times; but I don't want to complain, but endure cheerfully to the end. I am weak and weary, and have not recovered entirely from the wound. It is growing dark, and I must cook my supper. What shall I have? I guess I will cook a little hard-tack. Oh that I could have a good meal! For the last two days we have had no rations given out to us, and had to starve; but we draw rations this noon.

"Your loving soldier-brother,
"EDWARD."

On the 4th of June he writes from "Battlefield near Hanover town, or ten miles from Richmond":—

"MY DEAR LIZZIE,—I have just this minute received your letters of the 27th and 29th; and oh how glad I am to get them! They do me more good than anything else. I am well, but weak and faint. We have had hardly anything to eat since yesterday morning. I hourly expect to get something to eat. I wrote you last from near the North Anna River, after the battle. I am glad to be able to say that my wound is a great deal better. I was in the hospital about eight days, and got well enough to join my regiment on June 1st. That night or morning we were attacked by the rebs; but we were in the reserve, and not in much danger. The 2d (June 2d) we left our breastworks, and the rebels followed close on our heels, and attacked us, but were repulsed after some little sharp fighting. Here we had two of our company wounded. Yesterday, the 3d, we were under fire twice, at the time the rebels tried to turn our right flank; but they were repulsed twice. . . The 57th stood like a rock."

June 12th he writes from Athens Mill, Va.: —

"MY PRECIOUS SISTER A——, — Yesterday evening I was lying in my place, in the breastworks thinking of you, when the sergeant said, 'Fall in, Co. K, for your mail.' On going up to him, the first letter I saw was one from you to me,—the one you wrote from L. I also received the letter you wrote from E., accompanied with Lizzie's letter; and what a feast it was for me! They do me more good than anything else. When I received the sad news of James's death, I was at Mine Run, at the head-quarters of Maj. Gen. Crittenden, our division general having been detailed as his guard for a few days. I believe I received the news Friday. On Friday we drew two days' rations, which were consumed by Saturday night, and that evening we left Mine Run, (without rations), marched all night, marched all day Monday, and stood guard Monday night. All this I had to do with hardly anything to eat except three or four ears of corn and some coffee and a little piece of meat. But this was not the hardest. The death of James almost disheartened me. Tuesday we had the battle of North Anna River; I got tired of being on the general's guard, and joined my company and got wounded that day. My wound is almost well now; but I am entirely worn out, for we have been marching, fighting, and digging trenches for four weeks, and, at times, having to do this without anything to eat. If I could have three weeks' rest at Englewood, I think I could recruit enough to go in again for a month. But this cannot be, of course, unless I was wounded pretty badly; then I could get a thirty-days' furlough. What I need is *rest*. Oh, what meaning that word conveys to me! O A——, I want you to lean on me! If there is anything you wish that I can do, only say so, and I will try to fulfil your desire. I wish I could talk instead of write to you, for writing seems a poor substitute for talking. . . . I have been two months in the service now, and have seen pretty hard service, if I do have to say it. When I have been so weary and weak, I have longed to join James, and, perhaps, I shall soon. . . . I don't know as you are aware that I sent William Dwight four hundred dollars of my bounty money, and he is to put it at interest for me. I have decided, in case of my death, that Lizzie shall have two hundred dollars, and you two hundred. This, to me, is the best disposition that can be made of the money, in case of my death. I want to know how this suits you. Will you let me know?

I wrote you from Rappahannock Station, and I wrote Lizzie three letters from Spotsylvania, which have been lost, I fear. I was in three days of the fight at Spotsylvania Court House; was in the battle of North Anna River, and three engagements up here. God has been very gracious to me, and spared my life. I cannot be thankful enough to him for his goodness. To-day is Sunday. Oh how I would like to go to church with you! O A——! I long to see you, but I fear I can't for a long time to come, unless something turns up. . .

"Yours in haste, affectionately,
"EDWARD."

CHAPTER IV.

KILLED IN BATTLE.

HAVING copied this brief record of fighting in May and June, it is fit that we should take from the same source two entries more: —

June 16th. — " Determined attack on main rebel works at Petersburg, by Hancock, Smith, and Burnside, but with little success, and our loss some two thousand. Meanwhile, Butler sends out Terry with a force, which tears up two miles of railroad and cuts off Petersburg from Richmond for a day."

June 17th. — " Heavy fighting before Petersburg, — Burnside's troops assaulting and carrying an important part of the rebel main works about a mile and a half from the city, into which he threw a few shells. After several vain attacks during the day, the rebels recapture the works, however, after 9 p. m. Whole Union loss about twelve hundred."

It was in this last-named assault by Burnside's troops, June 17th,— the anniversary of the battle of Bunker Hill, — that young Schneider fell, mortally wounded. In making this assault, his courage and enthusiasm stimulated him to take a position which exposed him prominently to the fire of the enemy, and which was probably indiscreet on his part. But the loss was heavy on this day, as on the previous day, and, indeed, as it had been on the successive days of fighting, all the way from the beginning of the battle of the Wilderness ; and this exposure may or may not have been the occasion of his death. In this chapter we shall make use mainly of the writings of others, who were near at hand, or who were familiar with all the particulars at the time.

The chaplain of the 57th Regiment was Rev. A. H. Dashiell, Jr., and, immediately after young Schneider's death, he despatched a short note to Mrs. Dwight, his sister at Englewood, apprising her of the sad fact ; and as soon as he could secure the necessary leisure, he wrote her the following letter, giving the circumstances : —

KILLED IN BATTLE. 317

"Hospital of the 1st Division, 9th
Army Corps, near Petersburg.

"My dear Mrs. Dwight,— I promised, when I wrote briefly announcing Edward's death, to give you the particulars, so soon as I could find time for the purpose. Now, after burying those who were mortally wounded (thirty-eight), and sending off to Washington some six hundred more, I take the time to perform the sacred duty.

"It seems, from what I can learn, that Edward, when the order to charge the enemy's works was given, pushed on in advance of his company, determined to be the first to mount them, and when within a few paces of them, and ten feet ahead of his company, he fell, shot through the abdomen. As soon as he was brought to the hospital, he sent for me, and I did what I could for his comfort; though he and hundreds of others were obliged to lie on the ground as thick as autumnal leaves. The next day, when I could learn more accurately the nature of his wound, I discovered that it was mortal, and, when pressed by him to know what I thought, my tears revealed to him the truth. I thought of that sister who with tears had commended him to me, and that noble father far away, and I could not restrain them. Soon Dr. White, surgeon of the 57th Massachusetts, and Mr. Westwood came up and confirmed my opinion; and *he* expressed his hearty acquiescence in the will of God. The captain of his company came up; and when asked by Mr. W. what message the captain should bear back to his companions, he said, 'Tell them to stand by the dear old flag,' with a touching tenderness in his tone. When he was told that he had but a few hours to live, he looked up to me with a smile, and repeated the verse of a song which is sung by the soldiers: —

> " Soon with angels I'll be marching,
>   With bright laurels on my brow;
> I have for my country fallen,
>   Who will care for *sister* now ?"

" In the original lines it is *mother*. You understand the change. I put him in charge of my servant, as other duties called me away. In the evening he sent for me; indeed, poor fellow, I could not go near him without his calling to me. I was all he had to cling to of home and friends, except those he made at the time. I sat down by him in a Sibley tent, whither he had been removed, and he gave me these messages to you. First, he desired me to assure his father and you and all his friends that he died happy in the Lord, in the fulness of hope; to which I can bear testimony. His face shone like an angel's. God had been disciplining him and preparing him for glory, as I have remarked for weeks past, as we have passed through these terrible scenes of battle and suffering. He said that he had done his duty to his country, and felt happy in that, too. He then adverted to you and to A——; told me his relations to her,— the tenderness of his fraternal attachment to her; and desired me to request you to divide equally between yourselves his bounty-money. He wished twenty dollars of the money at the mission-rooms to be appropriated to the American Board, and ten dollars to the Christian Commission, to whose agents and delegates he felt great obligations for their kindness to him in the hospital. All the rest, with his back pay and the small sum he had with him, he directed should be possessed by you alone. He said that his brother William was well to do, and did not need it, and desired me to send him this message: 'Stand by the dear old flag, and cling to the cross of Christ.' My duties forced me away, and, leaving him in the care of young How, one of his comrades, slightly wounded, I saw him only for a moment during the night, though it was a late hour when I laid down in my blanket. Before dawn I was up, getting the wounded into wagons and ambulances, to be removed to City Point, and he sent me a message to come to him. I was so engaged that I could not go at the moment. I said, 'Presently.' In a few moments I went, and he was gone. I stood and wept. After breakfast I took my burying party and prepared the graves for many besides him; but I could not bury him in a trench with the rest, — so I dug his grave beside a tree, about a rod from the public road, and nailed a board, on which Mr. Westwood inscribed, 'Ed. M., son of Rev. Dr. Schneider, of Aintab, Turkey, of Co. K., 57th Mass. Reg't Inf.'; and, having enclosed the grave, I left him to await the great summons which is to awaken us all.

"He greatly impressed all who came near him, with the sweetness of his spirit, and the calm bravery with which he met death. I forgot to say that, when he requested me to publish a notice of his death, he wished me to understand that it was not to give notoriety to his name, but to acquaint his numerous friends of his death. . . . .

"Send this to your father, and believe me, in the tender bonds of which Edward is the link,

"Your brother in Christ,
"A. H. DASHIELL, JR.,
"Chaplain 57th Mass."

In a subsequent letter to Mrs. Dwight, Rev. Mr. Dashiell says: — "He was not alone when he died. Young How, a member of his company, slightly wounded, was with him. He sent for me when I was particularly engaged, about five minutes before his death, and could not leave; indeed, I did not suppose his end was so near. He saw me pass, and asked young How to call me. His sufferings were extreme. He did not talk very much; but I shall never forget the expression of those longing, loving eyes, when he would greet my coming. He seemed to love me with his whole heart because he had no one nearer to cling to."

Mr. Charles B. Newcomb, of Boston, employed at that time in the service of the Christian Commission, writes to Mrs. Dwight respecting her brother : — " I first became acquainted with your brother at Mount Carmel Church, where we halted one night on the march to the North Anna. There he was on guard, and his pleasant manner and the conscientiousness in the performance of his duty drew my attention; and being both Massachusetts boys, and nearly of an age, we early became acquainted. At the North Anna River, he was in camp for a few days, and I learned to know him better; and the more I knew him, the more I loved him. Shortly after, we moved on, and he was sent back with the wounded to the White House; but one day he passed me on the road, trudging along in the heat and the dust, smiling and happy, on his way to rejoin his regiment. The next time we met was at our hospital camp, in the woods before Petersburg; and there, on the morning of the 18th of June, I found Edward lying under a tree, torn and bleeding from his cruel wound, but just as calm and cheerful as when I saw him in health and strength but a few days before. Several times during the day I was with him; and when he told me that he was going home, and that he was not afraid to die, he seemed so strong and cheerful, I could not believe him so near his end. He asked me to be with him when he died, and told me, as I talked with him, that he did not know how he might feel when he approached the dark valley, but his Saviour seemed near to him, and he felt no fear. How strange it seemed, the next morning, when they told us that he died at three o'clock! [It was the same hour in the morning that James had passed away at Key West.] But we know the Good Shepherd led him safely through the 'dark valley;' and now he rests sweetly in the shadow of the woods, and his spirit rejoices with the Redeemer above. Often, as I passed his grave from day to day, did I think of his far-off sister, and wished that, for her sake, the precious remains might be laid near her. But brave men sleep around, and we may believe that the angel of the resurrection guards his resting-place. Nor will it be long before we are joined to those gone home, and unite with them in praising our Divine Master before the great white throne of the Eternal and Infinite Father. 'Until the day break and the shadows flee away,' let us be patient, faithful, comforted."

The following communication, from Rev. Addison P. Foster, of Lowell, will present some features of young Schneider's experience in the army, which are not anywhere else distinctly brought out; while the whole will be read with interest as a graphic narrative of events preceding and leading on to his death: —

"I first met Edward M. Schneider on the North Anna. It was in the last of May, 1864. Our army had passed down through Virginia, leaving the bloody battle-fields of the Wilderness and Spotsylvania behind; and here, on the banks of another river, there was a temporary halt, and, for a few days, some persistent skirmishing. In some one of these attacks upon the enemy, Schneider had been wounded in the knee, not severely, but painfully, so that he could scarcely walk. His chaplain, Rev. Mr. Dashiell, of Stockbridge, Mass., whose heroic fidelity to duty, and whose self-denying labors of love will long be remembered by all who were under his care, introduced him to the notice of our company of delegates, giving us something of his history, and assuring us there was not a more faithful Christian young man in all the regiment. We took him to our tent, and, while we refreshed him physically, we were refreshed spiritually. He spoke such earnest, modest, Christian words, that our hearts were stirred.

"A few days after, orders came for the hospital to prepare for the onward march, by sending all its wounded to Washington. It was Wednesday, the 26th of May. As those disabled by wounds or disease were being hurried into rough army-wagons for their transportation, we found Schneider sitting by the edge of the woods, and weeping bitterly. The surgeons, under a supposition that his pains were unreal, and his inability to walk pretended, had ordered him to shift for himself. They are not to be blamed for this, for Schneider's wound was not in appearance serious; they knew nothing of him, and they every day were sorely tried by soldiers who sought to skulk from duty by feigned misfortunes. Two of the delegates, who could certify to Schneider's worthiness, went to the surgeons with a statement of the case. On their representation, he was sent with the other wounded men to Port Royal, thence to be forwarded, as we supposed, to Washington.

"Several days passed. Our army, gathering itself up at Chesterfield like a huge serpent making ready for a spring, had uncoiled itself along the dusty roads that skirted the river,— had crossed the Pamunkey, and had come to another halt on the winding banks of the Tolopotomoy. Here, on Tuesday, the 1st of June (I am not positive as to the correctness of this date or of the preceding), I saw Edward again. I met him near our camp, begrimed with the dust of travel, loaded down with knapsack and gun, stepping somewhat feebly with his injured leg, and yet pressing forward with a bright, eager look upon his face, as if unconscious of fatigue.

"'Why, Edward!' I exclaimed; 'how is this? I supposed you were in Washington by this time.'

"'Well,' he replied, 'when I reached Port Royal, my knee was so much better that I thought I didn't need to go. I was anxious to get back to my regiment. I felt it to be my duty to join them if I could.'

"When he might have been resting comfortably in a northern city, enjoying a furlough, the noble boy had walked thirty miles and over, enfeebled by his wound, in the terrible heat of the opening summer, with every disadvantage of heavy equipments, had caught up with our advancing columns, and was then hastening to a post of hardship and danger.

"Once more I saw him. It was Friday night, the ever-memorable 17th of June. Our army had gone steadily southward. At Cold Harbor it had met with fearful losses; but, undiscouraged, it had thrown itself rapidly to the left of the enemy, and gained a foothold south of the James. We were now within two or three miles of Petersburg. The position had been secured by a forced march, beginning early Wednesday night, lasting through all those hours of darkness, and continuing, with scarcely a moment's rest, till late into Thursday afternoon. The Thursday's sun soon set, but the flash and glare of heavy guns struggled with the gloom till the break of day. The steady war of cannon and the fitful rattle of musketry allowed no sleep. With the morning dawn came the fearful crash and tumult of a battle begun in deadly earnest.

"The hospital with which our commission-wagon was stationed stripped itself for the work that all knew was coming. The place was cleared. Tents were improvised from every bit of canvas. All the stores and surgical instruments were brought out for immediate use. At noon the terrible procession began to come in. Ambulance after ambulance discharged its burden of wounded and dying men, and hastened back for more. The tents were quickly filled. The canvas coverings soon had their capacity tested to the utmost. And then, through that awful camp of death, the suffering soldiers were placed in rows on the bare ground, under the open canopy of heaven, in the chill night-air, till six hundred bleeding, groaning men lay crowded side by side. At last, about ten o'clock, the ambulances began to come in with only a single man in each. 'Thank God!' said the doctor who had been directing their unlading; 'now I know the wounded are almost all in.'

"That was a terrible night. All through those weary hours the noble surgeons toiled at their work. There lay these hundreds of suffering men, faint from loss of blood, having eaten nothing since morning, and now brought from the field without their blankets, while the hospital could not begin to supply the deficiency. Something must be done to sustain their lives till morning came. I was requested to give them all a small quantity of stimulant. While in this work, passing with great difficulty among the throng, one attracted my attention by lying quiet and uncomplaining, when very many were groaning loudly. At first, too, he refused to take the stimulant, and did not till I told him it was the doctor's order. As I bent down to him with the cup, he smiled faintly in recognition. 'Don't you know me?' he said. Swinging my lantern round so that its lurid light shone full on a bronzed face, now pale with exhaustion and loss of blood, I recognized him instantly. It was Schneider. 'Why, my dear Edward!' I exclaimed; 'are you here? Are you badly wounded?'

"I think so,' he replied; 'I should like to

have the doctor examine my wounds.' I hunted up Chaplain Dashiell, pointed out Schneider to him, requested him to procure a doctor, and left for a moment to complete my distribution. When I returned, the regimental surgeon, Dr. White, who was to the last tenderly kind to Edward, had just left, having made an examination. The chaplain, however, still remained, the tears falling silently upon his face. 'Oh,' he whispered to me, 'that poor boy will leave us soon! He is wounded in five places: his left arm is broken; his other arm is gashed by a bullet; his right hand is badly cut; there is a flesh-wound in his leg.* These might not be fatal; but, in addition, he is shot *through the bowels*, and the ball has lodged in the back.' I afterward learned that Edward had entered the battle burning with a desire to show himself no shirker. He had determined to be the first man of his regiment inside the rebel works. With eager foot he was pressing on ahead of all his companions; he was almost on the earthworks of the enemy, when he fell, mangled and bleeding, never again to rise.

* I do not feel positive as to the position and character of these three minor injuries.

"The chaplain and I stood for a moment without a word. It was a bitter thing to think that death must come and snatch this youthful hero from our sight. At length the chaplain broke the silence. 'Edward,' said he, in a trembling voice, 'I must tell you that you are mortally wounded. The doctor says you cannot live till morning. Do you feel ready to die?'

"At first the wounded boy made no reply; then, lifting his beautiful eyes towards us, he said: 'I came prepared for this. I love my Saviour and trust in him. He will take care of me now.' Perfectly calm and undisturbed, he received the news that he must die. He knew that such a message had no terrors for him.

"Another silence, and again he turned his head, and, looking steadily at us, he slowly repeated that touching verse, ending,—

"I have for my country fallen;
Who will care for sister now?'

He had in mind an adopted sister, the betrothed of his brother James, for whose protection and provision he was deeply anxious.

"The chaplain stooped down and took his pocket-book and other valuables. 'What message will you send home with these?'

"Tell my brother,' he answered, after a moment's thought, 'to stand by the dear old flag and cling to the cross of Christ.'

"Early the next morning, as soon as possible, Dr. White had Schneider put in the most pleasant spot in the Sibley tent. Every effort was made to secure his comfort. Soft boughs were placed under him for a bed, and he was wrapped warmly in hospital blankets. A little drummer-boy, slightly wounded, who was much attached to Edward, was permitted to sit by him and take care of him. He was plentifully supplied with lemonade and ice-water. These were the only things he could take into his stomach. Everything else produced, instantaneously, violent retching.

"He lay quite comfortable through the day. I visited him, for a moment at a time, every little while, as did also another member of the Commission.* Chaplain Dashiell was untiring in his attentions.

"Towards evening Schneider made his will. He left, of his little property, twenty dollars to the American Board, and ten dollars to the Christian Commission. He again expressed his

* Charles Newcomb, Esq., of Boston.

strong faith in his Saviour, and his willingness to meet death.

"About four o'clock on Sunday morning, June 19th, Chaplain Dashiell was busy on some errand of love, when a message came from Schneider, requesting to see him. The chaplain was compelled to delay a moment, and, when he entered the tent where Schneider lay, he found only an empty casket: the jewel, that adorned it, had been removed to shine in a more glorious setting.

"The burial was the same forenoon. The body was laid in a shallow grave, the face covered with a cloth. The chaplain and two or three of the Commission stood by. A prayer was offered, and the crumbling of the earth on an uncoffined corpse told us that all was over.

"Under a tall pine, close by the road between Petersburg and Prince George's Court House, is a grave distinguished from many others by a rude wooden railing about it, and by a board nailed to the tree, with this inscription:—

"'EDWARD M. SCHNEIDER,
OF AINTAB, TURKEY.
CO. K, 57th MASS. REGT.'"

Many are the noble-hearted young men who fell during those gloomy years of war,—youth of high culture and excellent promise. Many are the households that still go mourning over sons and brothers who went down in that long night of agony and blood. We make no invidious comparisons. We have aimed to tell the story of this young man, in the plainest and simplest way, as a thing by itself. It is not in our heart to detract in one iota from the noble deeds of others, or to undervalue the grief and loss of thousands of scattered households. This story may stand alone, as an illustration of what one young Christian patriot did and suffered for his country; and it was patriotism, pure and unalloyed, so far as we can judge, that moved him. He was not after office, or honor, or bounty-money. In all his long pleadings for permission to be a soldier, there is not a lisp of hoped-for promotion or earthly rewards. There was, also, apparently from the first, a kind of premonition what the end of all this would be. The very thought and feeling within him made him know, doubtless, that if he went into the army, he should go boldly, — go with a full purpose to shun no danger or personal exposure which would fall to his lot as a soldier. Feeling and knowing this, there was a kind of forecast that death was very likely to come to one who walked this perilous path; but, for all this, there was no drawing back, but ever an eagerness to press on. If genuine courage and patriotism are ever manifested among men, we think that the feelings which stirred in this young heart are fairly to be called by those names. How often are these virtues ascribed to men in conspicuous stations, — ascribed with lavish and fulsome words, — when, under such tests and trials as this youthful soldier went through, they would have been found utterly wanting!

How this young man grows upon us during the few years we have him directly under our eye! When he first came to our shores from his distant home, his impulses were in excess of his reason. He was but a boy, ruled largely by his fancies and his passions, — a constant source of anxiety to his friends. It was quite problematical what his life and character would be. But when the balance had been adjusted by the operations of the Holy Spirit upon his soul, the fickleness and blind impulse of the boy cease, and he begins to move before us with the dignity and concentrated force of a man. And from that day forward our respect for him constantly increases; and when, at last, the fatal day comes, we cannot but feel that a hero has died. Though young in years, and wearing only the uniform of a private, there is a certain greatness about those last months of his life, and the manner in which he met death. Strong and brave men pause involuntarily at such a spectacle, moved with profound homage and respect.

He was born on the 17th of August, 1846, and he fell, mortally wounded, on the 17th of June, wanting just two months of the military age. He left Massachusetts for the front on the 18th of April; so that in the short space of two months his whole work, as a soldier, was done.

We have not overrated the impression which his life and death made upon his military companions, upon his Christian instructors and guides, and upon the public at large, so far as the facts were known. When the news of his death reached Andover, as we learn from a letter of one of his school-companions, "the students of the Theological Seminary placed their flag at half-mast. At the Academy, Dr. Taylor, the Principal, made quite lengthy remarks upon his death and dying words, which were very affecting, — the doctor himself being moved to tears. Other marks of respect were paid to his memory."

At the time of young Schneider's death, Mr. C. C. Coffin ("Carleton"), was the army-correspondent of the "Boston Journal"; and the letter which he wrote soon after, and which was published in the "Journal," is such a just and beautiful tribute to his memory, that, though some things already recorded will be repeated, we give it entire: —

"IN MEMORIAM.

"While riding up from City Point to the front to-day, a friend, attached to the Christian Commission, pointed out a grave by the roadside, near the Fifth Corps hospital, about a mile east of the Dunn House. For me it had a special interest, as it will have for thousands, — the grave of Edward M. Schneider, 57th Mass.

When the regiment was formed, he was a student in Phillips Academy, Andover. From motives of patriotism purely, against the wishes of friends, he left the literature of the ancients, the history of the past, to become an actor in the present, and to do what he could for the future. His father is the well-known missionary of the American Board at Aintab, Turkey; and the son did what he thought would meet his approval.

"The chaplain of the regiment, Rev. Mr. Dashiell, has kindly given me information of what he has done for his country. On the march from Annapolis, he, though but seventeen years old, and unaccustomed to hardship, kept his place in the ranks, not once falling out, from the encampment by the waters of the Chesapeake to the Rapidan. He was slightly wounded on the North Anna, and was sent to' Port Royal for transportation to Washington, but of his own accord, returned to his regiment, joining it at Coal Harbor. While preparing for the charge upon the enemy's works, on the 17th, beyond the Dunn house, he said to the chaplain, 'I intend to be the first one to enter their works.'

"The charge was made. How grandly they moved through the woods! How quickly they swept up to the rebel line of defensive works, like an ocean billow upon a breakwater, rolling over it, engulfing all beyond! The brave young soldier tried to make good his words. With eager feet he led the advance, breaking out from the line and keeping a rod or two in advance.

"He was almost there, — not quite, — almost near enough to feel the hot flash of the rebel musketry in his face, — near enough to be covered with the sulphurous cloud from the cannon, — when he fell, shot through the body.

"He was carried to the hospital, with six hundred and fifty of his division comrades. He lay all night with his wound undressed, waiting his turn. There was not a murmur from his lips. The chaplain looked at his wound.

"'What do you think of it?' Seeing that it was mortal, he could not articulate a reply; neither could he restrain his tears. He remembered the last injunction of the young soldier's older sister: 'I commit him to your care.' The young hero interpreted the meaning of the tear — that his wound was mortal. 'Do not weep,' he said; 'it is God's will. I wish you to write to my father and tell him that *I have tried to do my duty to my country and to God.*' He disposed of his effects, giving ten dollars to the Christian Commission, twenty dollars to the American Board, and trifles to his friends. Then, in the simplicity of his heart, he said: 'I have a good many friends, school-mates and companions. They will want to know where I am, — how I am getting on. You can let them know I am gone, and that I die content. And, chaplain, the boys in the regiment, — I want you to tell them *to stand by the dear old flag!* And there is my brother in the navy, — write to him and tell him to *stand by the flag and cling to the cross of Christ!*'

" The surgeon came and examined the wound. 'It is my duty to tell you that you will soon go home,' he said.

"'Yes, doctor, I am going home. I am not afraid to die. I don't know how the valley will be when I get to it, but it is all bright now.' Then, gathering up his waning strength, he repeated the verse often sung by the soldiers, who, amid all the whirl and excitement of the camp and battle-field, never forget those whom they have left behind them, — mother, sister, father, brother. Calmly, clearly, distinctly, he repeated the lines, — the chorus of the song, —

> "'Soon with angels I'll be marching,
> With bright laurels on my brow;
> I have for my country fallen,
> Who will care for sister now?'

"The night wore away. Death came on apace. He suffered intense pain; but not a murmur escaped his lips. Sabbath morning came, and with the coming of the light he passed away. On the 17th of June, eighty-nine years ago, the sires of freedom freely gave their lives on Bunker Hill for the cause they loved. Not less worthy of remembrance are those who fell in front of Petersburg on this memorable day.

"Not many days hence a gray-haired man, far away in the Orient, will receive the tidings. The affliction may be severe; for, loving his work, serving his Master, he doubtless has looked down the vista of coming years, and beheld the boy succeeding him as a missionary of the Gospel; but in his affliction will he not thank God that he had such a son?

"He has not lived in vain. He has done his work, and has gone home to engage in a higher service. It was not for him to have all his heart's desire here, — to be the first to stand upon the rampart of the enemy's works, — but fearlessly and triumphantly he vanquished the last enemy, and came off a mighty conqueror.

"'I die content,' said the heroic and noble Wolfe, at Quebec, when told that the French were fleeing.

"'Stand up for Jesus,' said Dudley Tyng, in his last hours, — words which have warmed and moved thousands of Christian hearts.

"'Let me die with my face to the enemy,' was the last command of General Rice, the Christian, the soldier, the patriot, at Spotsylvania; but equally worthy of a place in the memories of men are the words of Edward M. Schneider, — the boy, the student, hardly eighteen years of age, the leader in the charge, — to his brother. They are the essence of all that Wolfe and Tyng and Rice uttered in their last moments. His grave is by the road-side, marked by a rude paling erected by Rev. Mr. Dashiell. The summer breeze sweeps through the sighing pines above the heaved-up mound. Mournful yet sweet the music of the wind-harp : mournful, in that one so young, so full of life, capable of such a future, should go so soon; sweet, in that he did his work so well. Had he lived a century, he could not have made it more complete. It was a short life, extending only from the peaceful shade of Old Andover to the intrenchment of Petersburg; but oh how full!

"I have given the record as narrated by his chaplain and by members of the Christian Commission, who were with him in his last moments. It is plain, simple, true. I am refreshed. The future is not dark. Will the tree of liberty become diseased and fall prematurely into the sear and yellow leaf, if nourished by such vital blood? No. There is compensation in God's economy. It is costly to sow such seed; but the return will be abundant, the harvest golden. Amid all the pain, the anguish, the tearing of heart-strings, waste and desolation of war, we have such compensation as this. There are thousands who are ready to follow where he marched to the cannon's mouth ; and there are other thousands, who have not yet taken their places in the ranks, young as he in years, who, as they read this record, will feel the patriotic flame kindling as never before.

"One week ago this Sunday morning, he passed, from the din of the dry, hot, dusty, bloody field of battle, to that land where peace floweth like a river for evermore. I have stood by the mouldering dust of those whose names are great in history, whose deeds and virtues are cut in brass and marble, who were reverenced while living and mourned for when dead ; but never have I felt a profounder reverence for departed worth than for him, — asleep beneath the pines, uncoffined, unshrouded, wearing, as when he fell, the uniform of his country. His last words — the messages to his comrades, to his father and his brother — will live so long as the flag of our country shall wave, or the cross of Christ endure. '*Stand up for the dear old flag and cling to the cross of Christ!*' They are the emblems of all our hopes for time and eternity. Short, full, rounded, complete, his life. Glorious such a death!

"CARLETON."

Many a worker in the Christian Commission, many a sun-browned soldier, has stopped to mourn over that quiet grave near the roadside at Petersburg.

A short time after his death, a writer — whom, from his signature, we understand to be A. D. F. Randolph, of New York city — published the following beautiful tribute to the young Christian patriot and hero, in the columns of "Harper's Weekly": —

"THE WORDS OF SCHNEIDER.

"ARMY OF THE POTOMAC, JUNE, 1864.

" We had crossed the Rappahannock,
  A hundred thousand men;
We had fought and flanked the foe, boys,
  And sent him to his den;
And of all who marched or skirmished,
  Of all who worked or fought,
Not one of the living or the dead
  · Had nobler aim or thought
Than he now sleeping yonder,
  Who challenged the foe at bay,

And stormed the works beyond the hill,
    And failed to win the day.

"He was nothing but a stripling,
    And, boys, I knew him well;
And they told his friends, — it soothed them,
    I was near him when he fell.
As the men were getting ready,
    With earnest voice he said,
'I am first the works to enter;
    I lead, and am not led.'
The line swept swiftly onward,
    And SCHNEIDER led the way:
He did not seize the roaring guns, —
    He talked with death that day!

"His father lives over the ocean, —
    He'd one son dead before, —
And the chaplain wrote the good old man
    That this one was no more.
And the boy, I watched beside him,
    With others brave as he,
But the words that passed his closing lips
    Ring out for you and me:
'*I tried to do my duty*
    To my country and my God.' —
O men at home! he, but a boy,
    For you this valley trod!

"More than this, my friends, he uttered;
    It sounded like a psalm;
And the angel watching in the tent
    Made everything so calm;

KILLED IN BATTLE.

'Now, dear chaplain,' said the hero,
  'My friends will want to know
How goes it; so tell 'em I have gone,
  And was content to go;
And, chaplain, tell my comrades,
  If the war should seem to drag,
I say to you, I say to them,
  STAND BY THE DEAR OLD FLAG.'

" Will you hear me further, comrades,
  Or have you heard enough?
No matter, Tom, the tears have come
  From some of sterner stuff.
He'd a brother in the navy,
  As brave, as true as he,
On the ocean, fighting rebel crews
  To make the ocean free!
'Now, chaplain, tell my brother,
  Though he suffer pain and loss,
To closely cling to the dear old flag,
  TO JESUS AND HIS CROSS.'

" Hearken to me still, my comrades;
  Sometimes there comes to me
A dream of the happy future years,
  And what is then to be:
Though it seems to come but slowly,
  God's day *is* drawing near,
When the rebel chiefs before the world
  Shall stand for judgment here.
This boy who died for freedom,
  Though a private — nothing more —
Shall live in contrast with the men
  That mankind will abhor!

> " O ye men who ne'er have spoken
>   A word for such as he,
> Who are plotting while we in the battle
>   Die that you may be free, —
> And ye whose Lord has been taken,
>   And laid you know not where !
> Let the words of this hero wake you
>   To watching and to prayer:
> ' *I have tried to do my duty*
>   *To my country and my God !* ' —
> O men ! O Christians ! rise and tread
>   The way this hero trod ! "

But this was sad news to go to that far-off, lonely missionary house in Aintab. Out of that little flock of five, that we saw together in Smyrna, in 1852, three have now gone. Death, that had for so many years spared the sacred enclosure of this Christian household, had now removed the mother and three of the children. Could these repeated griefs be borne ? The message of Edward's death was speedily communicated to Englewood, and Rev. Edward B. Dwight breaks the sad intelligence to his father. It is a long letter, and we have already quoted parts of it as better fitting an earlier stage of our narrative. That part which we now give is brief; but these opening sentences were sufficient to unfold the sad story to the waiting, anxious friends at Aintab. Mr. Dwight says: —

"MY DEAR FATHER, — God so wills it that our letters from here shall convey but the saddest tidings in these days. It is but a very few days since Harry (his brother) wrote to inform you of James's departure for a better world. Now another sorrow is burdening us. Eddie, too, has left us. A few days since, we saw the name of E. M. Schneider mentioned in the papers, among the wounded at the fierce assault upon the rebel works at Petersburg, but knew not of the extent of the wound until to-night. Now a letter has reached us from his chaplain, Rev. Mr. Dashiell, announcing his death."

We might, perhaps, conceive that no language could better express the feelings that would stir in that father's heart, far away, than those words, wonderful for their strength and concentrated energy, which Mrs. Browning puts into the mouth of the Italian mother, when the news came, first, that one of her sons had fallen in the cause of Italian liberty, followed almost immediately by the message that the other also had fallen: —

"Dead! one of them shot by the sea in the east,
    And one of them shot in the west by the sea!
Dead! both my boys! When you sit at the feast,
    And are wanting a great song for Italy free,
        Let none look at me.

. . . . .

"To teach them . . It stings then. *I* made them, indeed,
    Speak plain the word 'country'! *I* taught them, no doubt,
That a country's a thing men should die for at need;
    I prated of liberty, rights, and about
        The tyrant turned out.

"And when their eyes flashed . . O my beautiful eyes!
    I exulted! nay, let them go forth at the wheels
Of the guns, and denied not. But then the surprise,
    When one sits quite alone! Then one weeps, then one
        kneels!
        — God! how the house feels!

. . . . .

"Dead! One of them shot by the sea in the west,
    And one of them shot in the east by the sea!
Both! both my boys! — If, in keeping the feast,
    You want a great song for Italy free,
        Let none look at me."

But these words, wonderfully impressive though they may be, do not have the tone of that calm, quiet, Christian response which came back from Aintab. Dr. Schneider writes : —

"AINTAB, July 27, 1864.

"MY PRECIOUS DAUGHTER ELIZA, — Last Saturday evening, July 23d, came yours of June 23d, and William's of the 22d, announcing the fall of our dear Eddie. Of course it overwhelmed us. The first thing I read, on opening the letter, was his death. I cannot say that it was unexpected to me. From the day of the terrible battle on the North Anna River, I have been trembling for him; and then, as I followed the several battles that succeeded for some time, I was constantly in alarm lest he should be among the dead, wounded, or prisoners. My precious child! what shall I say, what can I say, to this double loss? Coming so soon after the other, it seems the more severe. My only refuge is the wisdom and mercy of God. I *know* that he doeth all things well, and that, even in our afflictions, he is aiming at our good. Painful as this fresh bereavement is, it must in some way work for our good, and must have been the best thing for our dear Eddie. Let us comfort ourselves with this assurance. The fact, that he was a Christian and a decided one, should assuage our grief. I remember how many are sacrificed in this war, who have not left behind them, for the consolation of their friends, such a hope. Ten thousands, all over our land, are mourning without such mitigations to their griefs. I am glad, also, that his precious remains were not buried promiscuously with others on the battle-field, but are where they can be distinguished from others. How glad I shall be to get the copy of his letter to you, in which he gives directions how to dispose of his little treasures; especially to get his dying messages from his chaplain! It is a great comfort to me, that he so favorably impressed that good man, and that there is so much reason to believe that his influence in the army was salutary and Christian. There are many other things, — many that should comfort us. Still a wave of desolation will sometimes come over me, and, I doubt not, over you. But we must look up: there is our comfort and hope. If these trials draw us nearer and nearer to God, and prepare us more and more for the heavenly world, they will not have been in vain to us. And, so far as we can comprehend, that is their aim.

"How eagerly we shall look for the next mail! It will bring us further particulars. Many and very precious letters of sympathy have come to us, and probably others will yet come. They give us great comfort.

"Your loving father,
"BENJAMIN SCHNEIDER."

By the same mail Mrs. Schneider writes; and a few sentences from her letter will help to reveal the state of thought and feeling in this distant missionary home : —

"AINTAB, July 27, 1864.

"MY DEAR ELIZA AND A——, — Let me tell you when there are chords of feeling touched that vibrate with keenest anguish, longing and ardent prayer. It is when your father, at morning worship, requests healing and strength and comfort '*for our dear daughters.*' Henceforth we cannot separate you. And so now, in our present distress, in our renewed sorrow, you are bound up in the same bundle of love. . . As I came in from our Saturday evening prayer-meeting, I saw that your father had returned from meeting the mail, and, with trembling feet, I walked up the steps to the study. On opening the door, the first look of your father revealed the fact. I asked no question. With trembling lips he uttered, 'He's gone! he's gone!' . . Miss Proctor, in speaking of him, last evening, referred to the account of Faithful's death. 'Now, I saw that there stood behind the multitude, a chariot and a couple of horses, waiting for Faithful, who was carried up through the clouds, with sound of trumpet, the *nearest way* to the celestial gate.'

"I dare not dwell on the *way* yet,— his sufferings those two days. But, oh! what reason for gratitude, that the chaplain was drawn to him; that he loved him, and took care of him! . . .

"Ever yours,
"Auntie."

Surely there is nothing in all this to forbid that Christian father from joining, with full heart and voice, in the "great song" for America "free." And though the voice may tremble while he sings, yet his soul is upborne with a fuller, nobler joy, because by a great price he has earned the right to rejoice.

In the narrative which is now finished, we have been passing through a changing scene of joy and sorrow, — pure and innocent joy mingled with keenest anguish. We have been led along a way of sharp and quick transitions, — bright and beautiful hopes suddenly dashed, — great plans frustrated. We have seen the pain that comes from the separation of households, even in this earthly life, and the more painful separation wrought by death. But, as we cast one glance backward, through it all and out of it all comes this conviction, that there is nothing on earth so beautiful as an earnest and well-spent Christian life. How noble and dignified is true Christian labor! What though it involves so much self-denial and sacrifice? What though the faithful servant of Christ must wear away his life "in journeyings often, in perils of waters, in perils of robbers . . in weariness and painfulness?" There is a high and sacred joy in the midst of it all, because God from on high looks down and says, " Well done, good and faithful servant." And then, beyond it all, when a few short years shall have rolled away, " there remaineth a rest for the people of God." There is a calm that comes after all these storms and agitations; there is security after these years of anxiety; there is rest after toil. " The burden and heat of the day" will soon be over, and the quiet evening will come on, when the weary ones shall be at rest.

"Upon the hills the wind is sharp and cold;
The sweet young grasses wither on the wold,
And we, O Lord, have wandered from thy fold;
But evening brings us home.

"Among the mists we stumbled, and the rocks
Where the brown lichen whitens, and the fox
Watches the straggler from the scattered flocks;
But evening brings us home.

"The sharp thorns prick us, and our tender feet
Are cut and bleeding; and the lambs repeat
Their pitiful complaints. Oh, rest is sweet
When evening brings us home!

"We have been wounded by the hunter's darts;
Our eyes are very heavy, and our hearts
Search for thy coming. When the light departs,
At evening bring us home.

" The darkness gathers. Through the gloom no star
Rises to guide us. We have wandered far;
Without thy lamp we know not where we are.
    At evening bring us home.

" The clouds are round us, and the snow-drifts thicken ;
O thou, dear Shepherd, leave us not to sicken
In the waste night, — our tardy footsteps quicken ;
    At evening bring us home." *

* Macmillan's Magazine.

www.ingramcontent.com/pod-product-compliance
Lightning Source LLC
Chambersburg PA
CBHW020241240426
43672CB00006B/602